Laboratory Manual

Prentice Hall
Earth
Science

PEARSON
Prentice
Hall

Boston, Massachusetts
Upper Saddle River, New Jersey

Laboratory Manual

Prentice Hall

Earth Science

Acknowledgments
Front Cover: Jim Lopes/Shutterstock; Page **DB2 (Crystals A, B, C and E),** Jeff Scovil/Scovil Photography;
DB2 (Crystal D), Charles D. Winters/Photo Researchers, Inc.; **DB3 (Crystal F),** Carolina Biological/Visuals Unlimited;
DB3 (Crystal G), Breck Kent/Earth Scenes; **DB3 (Crystal H),** José Manuel Sanchis Calvete/CORBIS; **DB3 (Crystal I),**
Gary Retherford/Photo Researchers, Inc.; **DB3 (Crystal J),** Jeff Scovil/Scovil Photography; **DB6–DB7,** David
Sandwell, Scripps Institution of Oceanography; **DB13,** Carrie Gowran; **DB16–DB17,** Unisys Corporation.

ISBN 0-13-362788-8

9 10 V011 18 17 16 15

Contents

SI Units and Conversion Tables ix

Student Safety Manual

Science Safety Rules x

Safety Symbols xiii

Laboratory Safety Contract xiv

Student Safety Test xv

Laboratory Skills Checkup 1
Defining Elements of a Scientific Method xix

Laboratory Skills Checkup 2
Analyzing Elements of a Scientific Method xx

Laboratory Skills Checkup 3
Performing an Experiment xxi

Laboratory Skills Checkup 4
Identifying Errors xxii

Laboratory Equipment xxiii

The symbol ⌂ denotes Design Your Own Experiment Lab

Laboratory Investigations

Introduction Investigations

Investigation A *Evaluating Precision* 1

Investigation B *Measuring Volume and Temperature* 7

Chapter 1   Introduction to Earth Science

Investigation 1A *The International System of Units (SI)* 11

Investigation 1B *Using a Topographic Map to Create a Landform* 17

Chapter 2   Minerals

Investigation 2 *Crystal Systems* 23

Chapter 3   Rocks

Investigation 3 *Classifying Rocks Using a Key* 31

Chapter 4   Earth's Resources

Investigation 4A *Recovering Oil* 37

Investigation 4B *Desalinization by Distillation* 41

Chapter 5   Weathering, Soil, and Mass Movements

Investigation 5 *Some Factors That Affect Soil Erosion* 47

Chapter 6   Running Water and Groundwater

Investigation 6A *Rivers Shape the Land* 53

Investigation 6B *Modeling Cavern Formation* 59

Chapter 7   Glaciers, Deserts, and Wind

Investigation 7 *Continental Glaciers Change Earth's Topography* 65

Chapter 8   Earthquakes and Earth's Interior

Investigation 8A *Modeling Liquefaction* 69

Investigation 8B *Designing and Building a Simple Seismograph* 73

Chapter 9   Plate Tectonics

Investigation 9 *Modeling a Plate Boundary* 79

Chapter 11   Mountain Building

Investigation 11 *Interpreting a Geologic Map* 85

Chapter 12   Geologic Time

Investigation 12 *Modeling Radioactive Decay* 89

Chapter 13   Earth's History

Investigation 13 *Determining Geologic Ages* 93

Chapter 14   The Ocean Floor

Investigation 14 *Modeling the Ocean Floor* 97

Chapter 16   The Dynamic Ocean

Investigation 16 *Shoreline Features* 101

Chapter 17   The Atmosphere: Structure and Temperature

Investigation 17A *Determining How Temperature Changes with Altitude* . . . 107

Investigation 17B *Investigating Factors That Control Temperature* 111

Chapter 18   Moisture, Clouds, and Precipitation

Investigation 18 *Recipe for a Cloud* 115

Chapter 19   Air Pressure and Wind

Investigation 19 *Analyzing Pressure Systems* 119

Chapter 20   Weather Patterns and Severe Storms

Investigation 20A *Analyzing Severe Weather Data* 123

Investigation 20B *Interpreting Weather Diagrams* 129

Investigation 20C *Creating a Weather Station* 133

Chapter 21   Climate

Investigation 21 *Modeling the Greenhouse Effect* 137

Chapter 22   Origin of Modern Astronomy

Investigation 22 *Measuring the Angle of the Sun at Noon* 141

Chapter 23   Touring Our Solar System

Investigation 23 *Exploring Orbits* 145

Chapter 24   Studying the Sun

Investigation 24 *Measuring the Diameter of the Sun* 151

Chapter 25   Beyond Our Solar System

Investigation 25 *Modeling the Rotation of Neutron Stars* 157

Student Edition Lab Worksheets

Chapter 1   Introduction to Earth Science

Exploration Lab

Determining Longitude and Latitude 161

Chapter 2   Minerals

Exploration Lab

Mineral Identification 165

Chapter 3   Rocks

Exploration Lab

Rock Identification 169

Chapter 4   Earth's Resources

Application Lab

Finding the Product That Best Conserves Resources 171

Chapter 5   Weathering, Soil, and Mass Movements

Exploration Lab

Effect of Temperature on Chemical Weathering 175

Chapter 6   Running Water and Groundwater

Exploration Lab

Investigating the Permeability of Soils 179

Chapter 7   Glaciers, Deserts, and Wind

Exploration Lab

Interpreting a Glacial Landscape 181

Chapter 8   Earthquakes and Earth's Interior

Exploration Lab

Locating an Earthquake 183

Chapter 9   Plate Tectonics

Exploration Lab

Paleomagnetism and the Ocean Floor 185

Chapter 10   Volcanoes and Other Igneous Activity

Exploration Lab

Melting Temperatures of Rocks 189

Chapter 11   Mountain Building

Exploration Lab

Investigating Anticlines and Synclines 191

Chapter 12   Geologic Time

Exploration Lab

Fossil Occurrence and the Age of Rocks 195

Chapter 13   Earth's History
Application Lab
Modeling the Geologic Time Scale 197

Chapter 14   The Ocean Floor
Exploration Lab
Modeling Seafloor Depth Transects 199

Chapter 15   Ocean Water and Ocean Life
Exploration Lab
How Does Temperature Affect Water Density? 203

Chapter 16   The Dynamic Ocean
Exploration Lab
Graphing Tidal Cycles 207

Chapter 17   The Atmosphere: Structure and Temperature
Exploration Lab
Heating Land and Water 209

Chapter 18   Moisture, Clouds, and Precipitation
Exploration Lab
Measuring Humidity 211

Chapter 19   Air Pressure and Wind
Exploration Lab
Observing Wind Patterns 215

Chapter 20   Weather Patterns and Severe Storms
Exploration Lab
Middle-Latitude Cyclones 217

Chapter 21   Climate
Exploration Lab
Human Impact on Climate and Weather 219

Chapter 22   Origin of Modern Astronomy
Exploration Lab
Modeling Synodic and Sidereal Months 223

Chapter 23   Touring Our Solar System
Exploration Lab
Modeling the Solar System 225

Chapter 24   Studying the Sun
Exploration Lab
Tracking Sunspots 227

Chapter 25   Beyond Our Solar System
Exploration Lab
Observing Stars 229

DataBank

Resource 1   Map Symbols DB1

Resource 2   Identifying Crystal Systems DB2

Resource 3   Earth's Tectonic Plates DB4

Resource 4   Global Bathymetry from Altimetry Data DB6

Resource 5   Ridge Fracture Zone DB7

Resource 6   Geologic Map of Devil's Fence, Montana DB8

Resource 7   Map Key for Geologic Map DB9

Resource 8   Topographic Map of Campti, Louisiana DB10

Resource 9   Topographic Map of Whitewater, Wisconsin DB11

Resource 10   The Geologic Time Scale DB12

Resource 11   Key to Index Fossils DB13

Resource 12   Atmospheric Temperature Curve DB14

Resource 13   Dew-Point Temperature Table DB15

Resource 14   Temperature Contour Plots DB16

Resource 15   Temperature Change and Heat Index Plots DB17

Resource 16   Some Common Minerals and Their Properties DB18

Resource 17   Classification of Rocks DB20

Resource 18   Topography of the Ocean Floor DB22

Resource 19   Star Charts DB24

Resource 20   Landforms of the Conterminous United States DB26

Resource 21   Circulation on a Rotating Earth/
Hertzsprung-Russel Diagram DB28

Resource 22   Middle-Latitude Cyclone Model DB29

Resource 23   Topographic Map of a Glacial Landscape DB30

SI Units and Conversion Table

COMMON SI UNITS

Measurement	Unit	Symbol	Equivalents
Length	1 millimeter	mm	1,000 micrometers (μm)
	1 centimeter	cm	10 millimeters (mm)
	1 meter	m	100 centimeters (cm)
	1 kilometer	km	1,000 meters (m)
Area	1 square meter	m^2	10,000 square centimeters (cm^2)
	1 square kilometer	km^2	1,000,000 square meters (m^2)
Volume	1 milliliter	mL	1 cubic centimeter (cm^3 or cc)
	1 liter	L	1,000 milliliters (mL)
Mass	1 gram	g	1,000 milligrams (mg)
	1 kilogram	kg	1,000 grams (g)
	1 ton	t	1,000 kilograms (kg) = 1 metric ton
Time	1 second	s	
Temperature	1 Kelvin	K	1 degree Celsius (°C)

METRIC CONVERSION TABLES

When You Know	Multiply by	To Find		
		When You Know	Multiply by	To Find
inches	2.54	centimeters	0.394	inches
feet	0.3048	meters	3.281	feet
yards	0.914	meters	1.0936	yards
miles	1.609	kilometers	0.62	miles
square inches	6.45	square centimeters	0.155	square inches
square feet	0.093	square meters	10.76	square feet
square yards	0.836	square meters	1.196	square yards
acres	0.405	hectares	2.471	acres
square miles	2.59	square kilometers	0.386	square miles
cubic inches	16.387	cubic centimeters	0.061	cubic inches
cubic feet	0.028	cubic meters	35.315	cubic feet
cubic yards	0.765	cubic meters	1.31	cubic yards
fluid ounces	29.57	milliliters	0.0338	fluid ounces
quarts	0.946	liters	1.057	quarts
gallons	3.785	liters	0.264	gallons
ounces	28.35	grams	0.0353	ounces
pounds	0.4536	kilograms	2.2046	pounds
tons	0.907	metric tons	1.102	tons

When You Know		
Fahrenheit	subtract 32; then divide by 1.8	to find Celsius
Celsius	multiply by 1.8; then add 32	to find Fahrenheit
Celsius	add 273	to find Kelvin

Science Safety Rules

To prepare yourself to work safely in the laboratory, read over the following safety rules. Then read them a second time. Make sure you understand and follow each rule. Ask your teacher to explain any rules you do not understand.

Dress Code

1. To protect yourself from injuring your eyes, wear safety goggles whenever you work with chemicals, flames, glassware, or any substance that might get into your eyes. If you wear contact lenses, notify your teacher.
2. Wear an apron or coat whenever you work with corrosive chemicals or substances that can stain.
3. Tie back long hair to keep it away from any chemicals, flames, or equipment.
4. Remove or tie back any article of clothing or jewelry that can hang down and touch chemicals, flames, or equipment. Roll up or secure long sleeves.
5. Never wear open shoes or sandals.

General Precautions

6. Read all directions for an experiment several times before beginning the activity. Carefully follow all written and oral instructions. If you are in doubt about any part of the experiment, ask your teacher for assistance.
7. Never perform activities that are not assigned or authorized by your teacher. Obtain permission before "experimenting" on your own. Never handle any equipment unless you have specific permission.
8. Never perform lab activities without direct supervision.
9. Never eat or drink in the laboratory.
10. Keep work areas clean and tidy at all times. Bring only notebooks and lab manuals or written lab procedures to the work area. All other items, such as purses and backpacks, should be left in a designated area.
11. Do not engage in horseplay.

First Aid

12. Always report all accidents or injuries to your teacher, no matter how minor. Notify your teacher immediately about any fires.
13. Learn what to do in case of specific accidents, such as getting acid in your eyes or on your skin. (Rinse acids from your body with plenty of water.)
14. Be aware of the location of the first-aid kit, but do not use it unless instructed by your teacher. In case of injury, your teacher should administer first aid. Your teacher may also send you to the school nurse or call a physician.
15. Know the location of the emergency equipment such as fire extinguisher and fire blanket.
16. Know the location of the nearest telephone and whom to contact in an emergency.

Heating and Fire Safety

17. Never use a heat source, such as a candle, burner, or hot plate, without wearing safety goggles.
18. Never heat anything unless instructed to do so. A chemical that is harmless when cool may be dangerous when heated.
19. Keep all combustible materials away from flames. Never use a flame or spark near a combustible chemical.
20. Never reach across a flame.
21. Before using a laboratory burner, make sure you know proper procedures for lighting and adjusting the burner, as demonstrated by your teacher. Do not touch the burner. It may be hot. Never

leave a lighted burner unattended. Turn off the burner when not in use.

22. Chemicals can splash or boil out of a heated test tube. When heating a substance in a test tube, make sure that the mouth of the tube is not pointed at you or anyone else.

23. Never heat a liquid in a closed container. The expanding gases produced may shatter the container.

24. Before picking up a container that has been heated, first hold the back of your hand near it. If you can feel heat on the back of your hand, the container is too hot to handle. Use an oven mitt to pick up a container that has been heated.

Using Chemicals Safely

25. Never mix chemicals "for the fun of it." You might produce a dangerous, possibly explosive substance.

26. Never put your face near the mouth of a container that holds chemicals. Many chemicals are poisonous. Never touch, taste, or smell a chemical unless you are instructed by your teacher to do so.

27. Use only those chemicals needed in the activity. Read and double-check labels on supply bottles before removing any chemicals. Take only as much as you need. Keep all containers closed when chemicals are not being used.

28. Dispose of all chemicals as instructed by your teacher. To avoid contamination, never return chemicals to their original containers. Never pour untreated chemicals or other substances into the sink or trash containers.

29. Be extra careful when working with acids or bases. Pour all chemicals over the sink or a container, not over your work surface.

30. If you are instructed to test for odors, use a wafting motion to direct the odors to your nose. Do not inhale the fumes directly from the container.

31. When mixing an acid and water, always pour the water into the container first then add the acid to the water. Never pour water into an acid.

32. Take extreme care not to spill any material in the laboratory. Wash chemical spills and splashes immediately with plenty of water. Immediately begin rinsing with water any acids that get on your skin or clothing, and notify your teacher of any acid spill at the same time.

Using Glassware Safely

33. Never force glass tubing or a thermometer into a rubber stopper or rubber tubing. Have your teacher insert the glass tubing or thermometer if required for an activity.

34. If you are using a laboratory burner, use a wire screen to protect glassware from any flame. Never heat glassware that is not thoroughly dry on the outside.

35. Keep in mind that hot glassware looks cool. Never pick up glassware without first checking to see if it is hot. Use an oven mitt. See rule 24.

36. Never use broken or chipped glassware. If glassware breaks, notify your teacher and dispose of the glassware in the proper broken-glassware container.

37. Never eat or drink from glassware.

38. Thoroughly clean glassware before putting it away.

Using Sharp Instruments

39. Handle scalpels or other sharp instruments with extreme care. Never cut material toward you; cut away from you.

40. Immediately notify your teacher if you cut your skin while working in the laboratory.

Field Safety

41. When leaving the classroom or in the field, do not disrupt the activities of others. Do not leave your group unless you notify a teacher first.

42. Your teacher will instruct you as to how to conduct your research or experiment outside the classroom.

43. Never touch any animals or plants that you encounter in the field unless your teacher instructs you in the proper handling of that species.

44. Clean your hands thoroughly after handling anything in the field.

End-of-Experiment Rules

45. After an experiment has been completed, turn off all burners or hot plates. If you used a gas burner, check that the gas-line valve to the burner is off. Unplug hot plates.

46. Turn off and unplug any other electrical equipment that you used.

47 Clean up your work area and return all equipment to its proper place.

48. Dispose of waste materials as instructed by your teacher.

49. Wash your hands after every experiment.

Safety Symbols

These symbols alert you to possible dangers in the laboratory and remind you to work carefully.

General Safety Awareness You may see this symbol when none of the symbols described below appears. In this case, follow the specific instructions provided. You may also see this symbol when you are asked to develop your own procedure in a lab. Have the teacher approve your plan before you go further.

Physical Safety When an experiment involves physical activity, take precautions to avoid injuring yourself or others. Follow instructions from the teacher. Alert the teacher if there is any reason you should not participate in the activity.

Safety Goggles Always wear safety goggles to protect your eyes in any activity involving chemicals, flames or heating, or the possibility of broken glassware.

Lab Apron Wear a laboratory apron to protect your skin and clothing from damage.

Plastic Gloves Wear disposable plastic gloves to protect yourself from chemicals or organisms that could be harmful. Keep your hands away from your face. Dispose of the gloves according to your teacher's instructions at the end of the activity.

Heating Use a clamp or tongs to pick up hot glassware. Do not touch hot objects with your bare hands.

Heat-Resistant Gloves Use an oven mitt or other hand protection when handling hot materials. Hot plates, hot glassware, or hot water can cause burns. Do not touch hot objects with your bare hands.

Flames You may be working with flames from a lab burner, candle, or matches. Tie back loose hair and clothing. Follow instructions from the teacher about lighting and extinguishing flames.

No Flames Flammable materials may be present. Make sure there are no flames, sparks, or other exposed heat sources present.

Electric Shock Avoid the possibility of electric shock. Never use electrical equipment around water, or when the equipment is wet or your hands are wet. Be sure cords are untangled and cannot trip anyone. Disconnect the equipment when it is not in use.

Breakage You are working with materials that may be breakable, such as glass containers, glass tubing, thermometers, or funnels. Handle breakable materials with care. Do not touch broken glassware.

Corrosive Chemical You are working with an acid or another corrosive chemical. Avoid getting it on your skin or clothing, or in your eyes. Do not inhale the vapors. Wash your hands when you are finished with the activity.

Poison Do not let any poisonous chemical come in contact with your skin, and do not inhale its vapors. Wash your hands when you are finished with the activity.

Fumes When poisonous or unpleasant vapors may be involved, work in a ventilated area. Avoid inhaling vapors directly. Only test an odor when directed to do so by the teacher, and use a wafting motion to direct the vapor toward your nose.

Sharp Object Pointed-tip scissors, scalpels, knives, needles, pins, or tacks are sharp. They can cut or puncture your skin. Always direct a sharp edge or point away from yourself and others. Use sharp instruments only as instructed.

Disposal Chemicals and other laboratory materials used in the activity must be disposed of safely. Follow the instructions from the teacher.

Hand Washing Wash your hands thoroughly when finished with the activity. Use antibacterial soap and warm water. Lather both sides of your hands and between your fingers. Rinse well.

LABORATORY SAFETY CONTRACT

I, _____ , have read the Science Safety Rules
and Safety Symbols sections on pages x–xiii of this manual, understand
their contents completely, and agree to demonstrate compliance with all
safety rules and guidelines that have been established in each of the
following categories:

(please check)

☐ Dress Code   ☐ Using Glassware Safely

☐ General Precautions   ☐ Using Sharp Instruments

☐ First Aid   ☐ Field Safety

☐ Heating and Fire Safety   ☐ End-of-Experiment Rules

☐ Using Chemicals Safely

Signature _____

Date _____

Name _____ Class _____ Date _____

Recognizing Laboratory Safety

Pre-Lab Discussion

An important part of your study of science will be working in a laboratory. In the laboratory, you and your classmates will learn about the natural world by conducting experiments. Working directly with household objects, laboratory equipment, and even living things will help you to better understand the concepts you read about in your textbook or in class.

Most of the laboratory work you will do is quite safe. However, some laboratory equipment, chemicals, and specimens can be dangerous if handled improperly. Laboratory accidents do not just happen. They are caused by carelessness, improper handling of equipment, or inappropriate behavior.

In this investigation, you will learn how to prevent accidents and thus work safely in a laboratory. You will review some safety guidelines and become acquainted with the location and proper use of safety equipment in your classroom laboratory.

Problem

What are the proper practices for working safely in a science laboratory?

Materials *(per group)*

Science textbook
Laboratory safety equipment (for demonstration)

Procedure

Part A: Reviewing Laboratory Safety Rules and Symbols

1. Carefully read the list of laboratory safety rules listed on pages x – xii of this lab manual.

2. Special symbols are used throughout this lab book to call attention to investigations that require extra caution. Use pages xii and xiii as a reference to describe what each symbol means in numbers 1 through 7 of Observations.

Part B: Location of Safety Equipment in Your Science Laboratory

1. The teacher will point out the location of the safety equipment in your classroom laboratory. Pay special attention to instructions for using such equipment as fire extinguishers, eyewash fountains, fire blankets, safety showers, and items in first-aid kits. Use the space provided in Part B under Observations to list the location of all safety equipment in your laboratory.

RECOGNIZING LABORATORY SAFETY (continued)

Observations

Part A

1. _____
_____
_____
_____

2. _____
_____
_____
_____

3. _____
_____
_____
_____

4. _____
_____
_____
_____

5. _____
_____
_____
_____

6. _____
_____
_____

7. _____
_____
_____

Name _____ Class _____ Date _____

RECOGNIZING LABORATORY SAFETY (continued)

Part B

_____

_____

_____

_____

_____

Analyze and Conclude

Look at each of the following drawings and explain why the
laboratory activities pictured are unsafe.

1. _____

_____

_____

_____

_____

_____

2. _____

_____

_____

_____

_____

_____

3. _____

_____

_____

_____

_____

_____

Name _____ Class _____ Date _____

RECOGNIZING LABORATORY SAFETY (continued)

Critical Thinking and Applications

In each of the following situations, write yes if the proper safety procedures are being followed and no if they are not. Then give a reason for your answer.

1. Gina is thirsty. She rinses a beaker with water, refills it with water, and takes a drink.

   _____

   _____

2. Bram notices that the electrical cord on his microscope is frayed near the plug. He takes the microscope to his teacher and asks for permission to use another one.

   _____

   _____

3. The printed directions in the lab book tell a student to pour a small amount of hydrochloric acid into a beaker. Jamal puts on safety goggles before pouring the acid into the beaker.

   _____

   _____

4. It is rather warm in the laboratory during a late spring day. Anna slips off her shoes and walks barefoot to the sink to clean her glassware.

   _____

   _____

5. While washing glassware, Mike splashes some water on Evon. To get even, Evon splashes him back.

   _____

   _____

6. During an experiment, Lindsey decides to mix two chemicals that the lab procedure does not say to mix, because she is curious about what will happen.

   _____

   _____

Laboratory Skills Checkup 1

Defining Elements of a Scientific Method

Laboratory activities and experiments involve the use of the scientific method. Listed in the left column are the names of parts of this method. The right column contains definitions. Next to each word in the left column, write the letter of the definition that best matches that word.

_____ **1.** Hypothesis	**A.**	Prediction about the outcome of an experiment
_____ **2.** Manipulated Variable	**B.**	What you measure or observe to obtain your results
_____ **3.** Responding Variable	**C.**	Measurements and other observations
_____ **4.** Controlling Variables	**D.**	Statement that sums up what you learn from an experiment
_____ **5.** Observation	**E.**	Factor that is changed in an experiment
_____ **6.** Data	**F.**	What the person performing the activity sees, hears, feels, smells, or tastes
_____ **7.** Conclusion	**G.**	Keeping all variables the same except the manipulated variable

Laboratory Skills Checkup 2

Analyzing Elements of a Scientific Method

Read the following statements and then answer the questions.

1. You and your friend are walking along a beach in Maine on January 15, at 8:00 am.

2. You notice a thermometer on a nearby building that reads −1°C.

3. You also notice that there is snow on the roof of the building and icicles hanging from the roof.

4. You further notice a pool of sea water in the sand near the ocean.

5. Your friend looks at the icicles and the pool and says, "How come the water on the roof is frozen and the sea water is not?"

6. You answer, "I think that the salt in the sea water keeps it from freezing at −1°C."

7. You go on to say, "And I think under the same conditions, the same thing will happen tomorrow."

8. Your friend asks, "How can you be sure?" You answer, "I'm going to get some fresh water and some salt water and expose them to a temperature of −1°C and see what happens."

Questions

A. In which statement is a prediction made?

_____

B. Which statement states a problem?

_____

C. In which statement is an experiment described?

_____

D. Which statement contains a hypothesis?

_____

E. Which statements contain data?

_____

F. Which statements describe observations?

_____

Laboratory Skills Checkup 3

Performing an Experiment

Read the following statements and then answer the questions.

1. A scientist wants to find out why sea water freezes at a lower temperature than fresh water.

2. The scientist goes to the library and reads a number of articles about the physical properties of solutions.

3. The scientist also reads about the composition of sea water.

4. The scientist travels to a nearby beach and observes the conditions there. The scientist notes the taste of the sea water and other factors such as waves, wind, air pressure, temperature, and humidity.

5. After considering all this information, the scientist sits at a desk and writes, "If sea water has salt in it, it will freeze at a lower temperature than fresh water."

6. The scientist goes back to the laboratory and does the following:

   a. Fills each of two beakers with 1 liter of fresh water.

   b. Dissolves 35 grams of table salt in one of the beakers.

   c. Places both beakers in a freezer at a temperature of −1°C.

   d. Leaves the beakers in the freezer for 24 hours.

7. After 24 hours, the scientist examines both beakers and finds the fresh water to be frozen. The salt water is still liquid.

8. The scientist writes in a notebook, "It appears that salt water freezes at a lower temperature than fresh water does."

9. The scientist continues, "I suggest that the reason sea water freezes at a lower temperature is that sea water contains dissolved salts, while fresh water does not."

Questions

A. Which statement(s) contain conclusions? _____

B. Which statement(s) contains a hypothesis? _____

C. Which statement(s) contain observations? _____

D. Which statement(s) describe an experiment? _____

E. In which statement is the problem described? _____

F. Which statement(s) contain data? _____

G. Which is the manipulated variable in the experiment? _____

H. What is the responding variable in the experiment? _____

Laboratory Skills Checkup 4

Identifying Errors

Read the following paragraph and then answer the questions.

Andrew arrived at school and went directly to his earth science class. He took off his cap and coat and sat down at his desk. His teacher gave him a large rock and asked him to find its density. Realizing that the rock was too large to work with, Andrew got a hammer from the supply cabinet and hit the rock several times until he broke off a chip small enough to work with. He partly filled a graduated cylinder with water and suspended the rock in the water. The water level rose 2 cm. Andrew committed this measurement to memory. He next weighed the rock on a balance. The rock weighed 4 oz. Andrew then calculated the density of the rock as follows: He divided 2 cm by 4 oz. He then reported to his teacher that the density of the rock was 0.5 cm/oz.

Questions

1. What safety rule(s) did Andrew break?

_____

_____

2. What mistake did Andrew make using measurement units?

_____

_____

3. What should Andrew have done with his data rather than commit them to memory?

_____

_____

4. What is wrong with the statement "He next weighed the rock on a balance"?

_____

_____

5. Why is "4 oz" an inappropriate measurement in a science experiment?

_____

_____

6. What mistake did Andrew make in calculating density?

_____

_____

Some Common Laboratory Equipment

test tube

test-tube rack

spatula

scoop

test-tube holder

rubber stoppers

tongs

forceps

well plates
(24- and 96-well)

spring scale

magnetic
compass

stopwatch

magnifying
glass

triple-beam balance

SOME COMMON LABORATORY EQUIPMENT (continued)

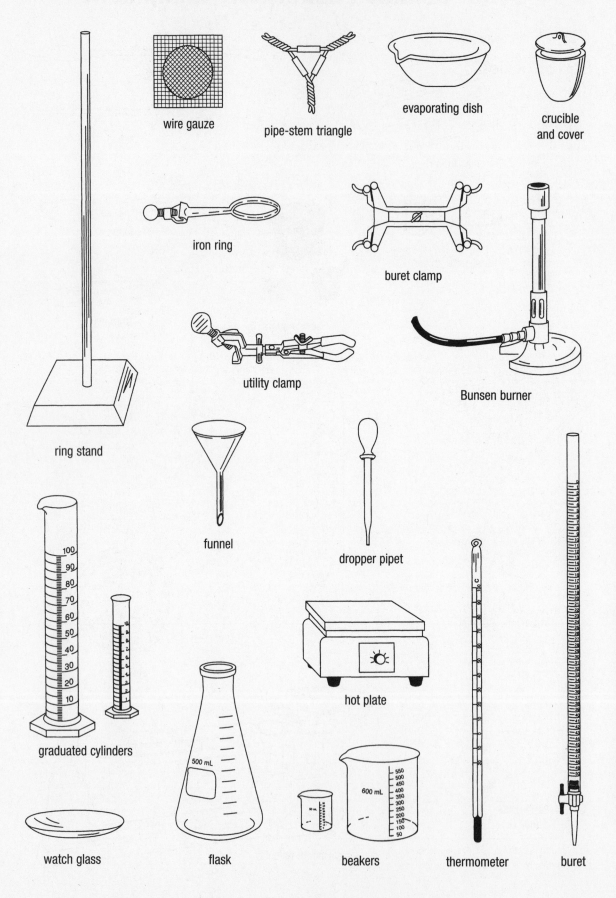

wire gauze

pipe-stem triangle

evaporating dish

crucible and cover

iron ring

buret clamp

utility clamp

Bunsen burner

ring stand

funnel

dropper pipet

hot plate

graduated cylinders

watch glass

flask

beakers

thermometer

buret

Name _____   Class _____   Date _____

Evaluating Precision

Introduction

When an object is measured more than once, the measurements may vary. The closeness of a set of measured values to each other is called **precision.** Many people confuse precision with accuracy. **Accuracy** is a measure of how close the values are to the actual value. A set of values can be in close agreement, or precise, without being accurate.

For example, suppose you repeatedly measure the mass of a 4.00-g mineral sample by using a balance that reads too low by 3.00 g every time. You might get nearly identical readings—for example, 1.00 g, 1.01 g, and 0.99 g. These readings are quite precise because they are close together. However, they differ from the actual value by a large amount. Therefore, the measurements are very inaccurate.

In this investigation, you will make several measurements of length, temperature, and volume. Then, you will evaluate the precision of your measurements by comparing them to measurements made by your classmates.

Problem

How can you determine the precision and accuracy of measurements?

Pre-Lab Discussion

Read the entire investigation. Then work with a partner to answer the following questions.

1. **Applying Concepts** Use the example of a series of repeated length measurements to explain the meaning of precision.

   _____

   _____

   _____

   _____

   _____

2. **Inferring** What information would you need to determine the accuracy of a measurement?

   _____

   _____

   _____

   _____

   _____

Name _____ Class _____ Date _____

3. Drawing Conclusions In this investigation, you will compare measurements that you make to measurements that your classmates make. Will you do this to determine the accuracy or the precision of your measurements?

_____

_____

_____

_____

4. Designing Experiments Identify the manipulated, responding, and controlled variables in this investigation.

   a. Manipulated variable

   _____

   _____

   _____

   b. Responding variable

   _____

   _____

   _____

   c. Controlled variables

   _____

   _____

   _____

5. Analyzing Data Two students measure the mass of a wooden disk, using the same balance. The first student repeats the weighing three times and obtains mass readings of 47 g, 52 g, and 51 g. The second student obtains mass readings of 45 g, 55 g, and 50 g. Explain which set of measurements is more precise. Can you tell if the measurements are accurate? Why or why not?

_____

_____

_____

_____

_____

_____

Materials *(per group)*

meter stick

Celsius thermometer

500-mL beaker filled with room-temperature water

10 pennies

50-mL graduated cylinder

Safety 🔲 🎽 🧤 🔥

Put on safety goggles and a lab apron. Be careful to avoid breakage when working with glassware. Note all safety alert symbols next to the steps in the Procedure and review the meaning of each symbol by referring to the Safety Symbols on page xiii.

Procedure

1. You and your partner make up a team. Your team and two other teams will make up a group of six. Your teacher will tell you and your partner whether you are Team A, B, or C of your group. The three teams in your group will measure the same objects separately. You will not share your measurements with the other teams in your group until you complete the procedure.

🎽 2. Working with your partner, use the meter stick to measure the length of a desk indicated by your teacher. Measure as carefully as possible, to the nearest millimeter. Record the length of the desk in the Data Table. (*Hint:* Do not reveal the measurements you make to the other teams in your group. They must make the same measurements and must not be influenced by your results.)

🧤 3. Use the thermometer to measure the temperature of the
🔥   beaker of room-temperature water. **CAUTION:** *Do not let the thermometer touch the beaker.* Record this measurement in the Data Table.

4. Place 25 mL of tap water in the graduated cylinder. Measure the volume of the water. Record this volume in the Data Table to the nearest 0.1 mL. (*Hint:* Remember to read the volume at the bottom of the meniscus.)

5. Add the 10 pennies to the graduated cylinder. Read the volume of the water and pennies. Record the volume the nearest 0.1 mL in the Data Table.

6. Subtract the volume of the water from the volume of the water and pennies. The result is a measurement of the volume of the pennies. Record this value in the Data Table.

7. After all three teams in your group have finished measuring the same objects for length, temperature, and volume, share your results with the other two teams. Record their measurements in the Data Table.

Name _____ Class _____ Date _____

Observations

DATA TABLE

Measurement	Team A	Team B	Team C
Length of desk (mm)			
Temperature of water (°C)			
Volume of water (mL)			
Volume of water and pennies (mL)			
Volume of pennies (mL)			

Analysis and Conclusions

1. **Calculating** Average the three length measurements you compared by adding them together and dividing the result by 3. Find the range of values by calculating the difference between the largest and smallest values. Record the results of your calculations in the space below.

   a. Average of length measurements (mm)

   _____

   b. Range of length measurements (mm)

   _____

2. Making Generalizations Would it be correct to use the range of values you calculated in Question 1 to describe the precision of the measurements? The accuracy of the measurements? Explain your answer.

_____

_____

_____

_____

_____

_____

_____

3. Analyzing Data Which of the three sets of measurements had the least spread among the measurements? Suggest reasons for the precision of these measurements.

_____

_____

_____

_____

_____

_____

4. Applying Concepts Figure 1 shows the results of three people's attempts to shoot as many bull's-eyes as possible. Below Figure 1, label each of the results as *accurate* or *not accurate*, and as *precise* or *not precise*.

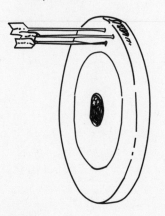 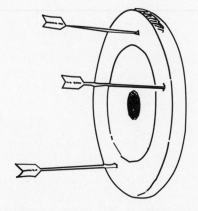 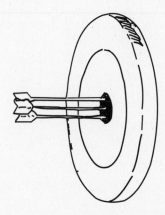

Figure 1

_____   _____   _____

_____   _____   _____

5. Evaluating and Revising Discuss the reasons for the differences among the teams' measurements with the members of your group. Describe these reasons and explain how the measurements could be made more precise.

_____

_____

_____

_____

_____

_____

_____

_____

Go Further

Design an experiment to compare the precision of two or more measuring instruments. Is the precision of each instrument the same throughout its range of measurements? Write a procedure you would follow to answer these questions. After your teacher approves your procedure, carry out the experiment and report your results.

Science Skills   **Introduction Investigation B**

Measuring Volume and Temperature

Introduction

The amount of space an object takes up is called its volume.
A commonly used unit of volume is the liter (L). Smaller volumes can
be measured in milliliters (mL). One milliliter is equal to 1/1000 of a
liter. In the laboratory, the graduated cylinder is often used to measure
the volume of liquids.

Temperature is measured with a thermometer. One unit of
measurement for temperature is the degree Celsius (°C).

In this investigation, you will practice making measurements of
the volume and temperature of a liquid.

Problem

How can you accurately measure the volume and temperature
of a liquid?

Pre-Lab Discussion

*Read the entire investigation. Then work with a partner to answer the
following questions.*

1. **Measuring** How many significant figures are there in the
   measurement shown in Figure 1?

   _____

2. **Inferring** Why is it important to read the volume of water in a
   graduated cylinder by using the bottom of the meniscus?

   _____

   _____

   _____

3. **Designing Experiments** Why should you leave the thermometer in
   beaker B when you add ice?

   _____

   _____

   _____

   _____

4. **Measuring** If each mark on a thermometer represents 1°C, which
   part of a temperature measurement will be the estimated digit?

   _____

   _____

Name _____ Class _____ Date _____

Materials (per group)

2 150-mL beakers   2 Celsius thermometers
100-mL graduated cylinder   watch or clock
glass-marking pencil   ice cube

Safety 🖐🦺🔥

Put on safety goggles and a lab apron. Be careful to avoid breakage
when working with glassware. Note all safety alert symbols next to
the steps in the Procedure and review the meaning of each symbol by
referring to the Safety Symbols on page xiii.

Procedure

Part A: Measuring the Volume of a Liquid

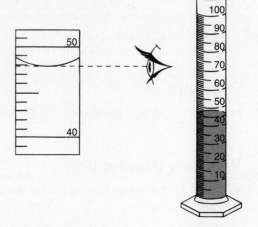

Figure 1

🔥 1. Fill a beaker halfway with water.

2. Pour the water in the beaker into the
   graduated cylinder.

3. Measure the amount of water in the
   graduated cylinder. To accurately measure
   the volume, your eye must be at the same
   level as the bottom of the meniscus, as
   shown in Figure 1. The meniscus is the
   curved surface of the water.

4. Estimate the volume of water to the nearest 0.1 mL. Record this
   volume in Data Table 1.

5. Repeat Steps 1 through 4, but this time fill the beaker only one-
   fourth full of water.

Part B: Measuring the Temperature of a Liquid

6. Use the glass-marking pencil to label the beakers *A* and *B*.

7. Use the graduated cylinder to put 50 mL of water in each
   beaker.

8. Place a thermometer in each beaker. In Data Table 2, record
   the temperature of the water in each beaker.

9. Carefully add one ice cube to the water in beaker B. Note and
   record the time.

10. After 1 minute, observe the temperature of the water in each
    beaker. Record these temperatures in Data Table 2.

11. After 5 minutes, observe the temperature of the water in each
    beaker. Record these temperatures in Data Table 2.

12. After the ice in beaker B has melted, use the graduated cylinder
    to find the volume of water in each beaker. Record these
    volumes in Data Table 3.

Name _____ Class _____ Date _____

Observations

DATA TABLE 1

Measurement	Volume of Water (mL)
Half-filled beaker	
One-fourth filled beaker	

DATA TABLE 2

Beaker	Temperature at Beginning	Temperature After 1 Minute (°C)	Temperature After 5 Minutes (°C)
A			
B			

DATA TABLE 3

Beaker	Volume of Water at Beginning (mL)	Volume of Water at End (mL)
A		
B		

Analysis and Conclusions

1. **Observing** What is the largest volume of a liquid that the graduated cylinder is able to measure? What is the smallest volume that the graduated cylinder is able to measure?

_____

_____

2. **Analyzing Data** Describe how the temperature of the water in beakers A and B changed during the investigation.

_____

_____

_____

_____

3. **Analyzing Data** How did the volume of water in beakers A and B change during the investigation? What do you think caused this change?

_____

_____

_____

_____

4. **Applying Concepts** Would you use a 100-mL graduated cylinder, a 25-mL graduated cylinder, or 10-mL graduated cylinder to measure 8 mL of a liquid? Explain your answer.

_____

_____

_____

_____

Go Further

Some liquids do not form a meniscus in a graduated cylinder as water does. Use a 10-mL graduated cylinder to measure 8.0 mL each of water, isopropyl (rubbing) alcohol, and vegetable oil. Observe and draw the meniscus of each liquid. Label your drawings to show how you think the volume of each liquid should be measured. Explain why you think that the volumes should be measured in this way.

The International System of Units (SI)

Introduction

Earth science, the study of Earth and its neighbors in space, involves investigations of natural objects that range in size from the very smallest parts of an atom to the largest galaxy. To measure and describe objects here on Earth as well as those far from our planet, Earth scientists use the **International System of Units (SI),** which is a decimal system of weights and measures. The base units of this system are shown in Data Table 1 on the next page. **Length,** which is the distance between two points, is measured in meters (m). The quantity of matter in an object, or **mass,** is measured in kilograms (kg). The amount of a substance is measured in **moles** (mol). The SI unit used to measure time is the second (s), and the unit for temperature is kelvins (K). Electric current is measured in units called amperes (A), and luminous intensity is measured in candelas (cd). Derived SI units, which are formed from combinations of the base units, are also shown in Data Table 1.

Prefixes are added to SI base units to indicate how many times more or what fraction of the base unit is present. For example, one thousand meters is a kilometer (km). One-thousandth of a meter is a millimeter (mm). Common metric prefixes and their symbols are shown in Data Table 2 on the next page.

To convert one SI unit into another, you simply move the decimal point either to the left or to the right. If you are changing a smaller unit into a larger unit, the decimal point is moved to the left. If you are converting a larger unit into a smaller unit, the decimal point is moved to the right. Figure 1 can be used to determine how many places the decimal point is moved during a conversion.

In this investigation, you will make measurements using SI units and convert SI units.

Problem

What are common SI units, and how can they be converted and compared to other units of measure?

Pre-Lab Discussion

Read the entire investigation. Then work with a partner to answer the following questions.

1. **Measuring** Which SI unit would you use to measure the amount of juice in a glass?

   _____

2. Comparing and Contrasting Which is larger—143.0 millimeters or 143.0 decimeters?

_____

3. Calculating How many millimeters are 1.43 decimeters?

_____

4. Calculating The average human body temperature in degrees Fahrenheit is 98.6. Use the Metric Conversion Table in the front of this manual to convert this value to degrees Celsius. Show your work.

DATA TABLE 1

SI Base Units			Derived Units		
Quantity	Unit	Symbol	Quantity	Unit	Symbol
Length	meter	m	Area	square meter	m^2
Mass	kilogram	kg	Volume	cubic meter	m^3
Temperature	kelvin	K	Density	kilograms per cubic meter	kg/m^3
Time	second	s	Pressure	pascal ($kg/m \cdot s^2$)	Pa
Amount of substance	mole	mol	Energy	joule ($kg \cdot m^2/s^2$)	J
Electric current	ampere	A	Frequency	hertz (1/s)	Hz
Luminous intensity	candela	cd	Electric charge	coulomb ($A \cdot s$)	C

DATA TABLE 2

Prefixes and Symbols		
Prefix[1]	Symbol[2]	Meaning
giga-	G	one billion times base unit (1,000,000,000 × base)
mega-	M	one million times base unit (1,000,000 × base)
kilo-	k	one thousand times base unit (1000 × base)
hecto-	h	one hundred times base unit (100 × base)
deka-	da	ten times base unit (10 × base)
deci-	d	one-tenth times base unit (0.1 × base)
centi-	c	one-hundredth times base unit (0.01 × base)
milli-	m	one-thousandth times base unit (0.001 × base)
micro-	μ	one-millionth times base unit (0.000001 × base)
nano-	n	one-billionth times base unit (0.000000001 × base)

[1]A prefix is added to the base unit to indicate how many times more, or what fraction of, the base unit is present.
For example, a kilometer (km) means one thousand meters and a millimeter (mm) means one-thousandth of a meter.
[2]When writing in the SI system, periods are not used after the unit symbols and symbols are not made plural.
For example, if the length of a stick is 50 centimeters, it would be written as "50 cm" (not "50 cm." or "50 cms").

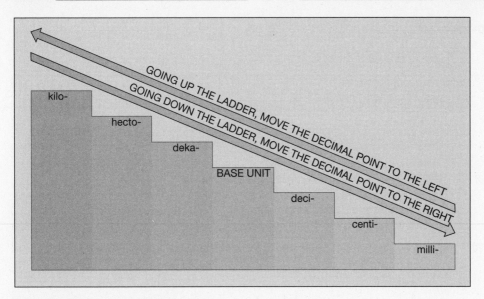

kilo-

hecto-

deka-

BASE UNIT

deci-

centi-

milli-

GOING UP THE LADDER, MOVE THE DECIMAL POINT TO THE LEFT

GOING DOWN THE LADDER, MOVE THE DECIMAL POINT TO THE RIGHT

Figure 1 Metric Conversion Diagram

Materials *(per group of students)*
metric ruler

metric tape measure or meter stick

paper clip

nickel

paper cup

small rock

laboratory balance

large graduated cylinder

calculator

Metric Conversion Tables on page ix in this manual

Safety 🖐

Be careful to avoid breakage when working with glassware.

Procedure
1. Work with a partner. Use the measuring tape or meter stick to measure either your height or your partner's height as accurately as possible to the nearest hundredth of a meter, or centimeter. Record your value in Data Table 3.

2. Change your value from Step 1 from centimeters to meters. Record this value in column 4 in Data Table 3. Use your calculator if necessary.

3. Repeat Steps 1 and 2 for all other measurements listed in Data Table 3 using the appropriate measuring device.

4. Use your data, the Metric Conversion Tables, and Figure 1 to answer the questions in the **Analysis and Conclusions** section.

Observations

DATA TABLE 3

Height (cm)		Height (m)	
Length of page (cm)		Length of page (mm)	
Length of shoe (mm)		Length of shoe (m)	
Length of paper clip (mm)		Length of paper clip (km)	
Diameter of coin (mm)		Diameter of coin (μm)	
Volume of paper cup (mL)		Volume of paper cup (L)	
Volume of rock (mL)		Volume of rock (μL)	
Mass of paper clip (g)		Mass of paper clip (μg)	
Mass of paper cup (g)		Mass of paper cup (kg)	
Mass of coin (g)		Mass of coin (cg)	
Mass of rock (g)		Mass of rock (kg)	

Name _____ Class _____ Date _____

Analysis and Conclusions

1. Calculating Use Figure 1 to make the following conversions.

    a. 2.05 meters (m) = _____ centimeters (cm)

    b. 1.50 meters (m) = _____ millimeters (mm)

    c. 9.81 liters (l) = _____ deciliters (dL)

    d. 5.4 grams (g) = _____ milligrams (mg)

    e. 6.8 meters (m) = _____ kilometers (km)

    f. 4214.6 centimeters (cm) = _____ meters (m)

    g. 321.50 grams (g) = _____ kilograms (kg)

    h. 70.73 hectoliters (hL) = _____ dekaliters (daL)

2. Calculating Use the information on page ix in this manual to make the following conversions.

    a. On a cold day it was 8°F, or _____ °C.

    b. Ice melts at 0°C, which is _____ °F.

    c. Room temperature is 72°F, or _____ °C.

    d. On a hot summer day, the temperature was 35°C, which is _____ °F.

    e. Water temperature in a warm shower is 27°C, or _____ °F.

    f. Hot soup can be 72°C, which is _____ °F.

    g. Water boils at 212°F, or _____ K.

Work Space for Calculations

3. **Analyzing Data** Use what you have learned about SI and the data you collected during this investigation to answer each of the following questions.

   a. The outdoor thermometer reads 28°C. Will you need your winter coat? _____

   b. If your body temperature is 40°C, do you have a fever? _____

   c. The thermostat in your classroom reads 37°C. Are you shivering or perspiring? _____

   d. Can an average man weigh 90 kilograms? _____

   e. About how many meters tall is a fire hydrant? _____

   f. Can one person drink 250 mL of coffee at breakfast? _____

   g. What is average room temperature in K? _____

   h. About how thick is a dime? _____

   i. Can a typical bathtub hold 80 liters of water? _____

   j. Can a pork roast that weighs 18 grams feed a family of four? _____

4. **Inferring** Explain why you think SI is used by most scientists around the world.

   _____

   _____

   _____

   _____

   _____

Using a Topographic Map to Create a Landform

Introduction

One of the many tools used to study Earth's landscape is a **topographic map,** which represents Earth's three-dimensional surface in two dimensions. Topographic maps use **contour lines** to show **elevation,** or height above sea level, on a two-dimensional surface. A **contour line** joins points on a map that have the same elevation. Contour lines never intersect. The difference in elevation between one contour line and the next contour line is the **contour interval.**

In this investigation, you will interpret the contour lines on part of a topographic map and use them to create a three-dimensional model, or landform.

Problem

How can you use a topographic map to create a landform?

Pre-Lab Discussion

Read the entire investigation. Then work with a partner to answer the following questions.

1. **Applying Concepts** How does a topographic map show the elevation of the land?

_____

_____

_____

_____

2. **Forming Operational Definitions** In your own words, define the term *contour interval.*

_____

_____

_____

3. **Inferring** Why can contour lines never intersect?

_____

_____

_____

_____

4. Interpreting Diagrams/Photographs What kind of topography is indicated by contour lines that are very close together? By contour lines that are very far apart?

_____

_____

_____

_____

5. Using Models What is the advantage of creating a landform from a topographic map?

_____

_____

_____

_____

Materials *(per group)*

transparent shoebox with lid

nonpermanent, fine-lined marking pen

enlarged photocopy of part of a topographic map

cellophane or masking tape

modeling clay

metric ruler

Procedure

1. Place the topographic map provided by your teacher inside the lid of the plastic box so that the map can be seen through the top of the lid. Secure the map to the lid by using small pieces of tape near the map's corners.

2. Place the lid on your desktop or table. Use the nonpermanent marking pen to trace the topographic map onto the box lid. When you have finished tracing every contour line, remove the map from the inside of the lid and put the lid aside.

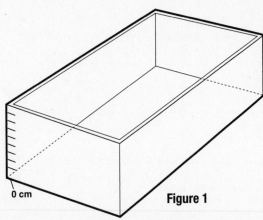

Figure 1

0 cm

3. Use the marking pen and the metric ruler to make a centimeter scale along one of the vertical sides of the box, as shown in Figure 1.

4. Find the lowest elevation on the topographic map provided by your teacher. Write this elevation next to the bottom edge of the box.

5. Determine the contour interval of your topographic map. Each centimeter mark on the side of the box will represent the same vertical distance as the contour interval. Next to each centimeter mark, write the actual elevation in meters.

6. Use the modeling clay to make the first layer of the landform on your topographic map.

7. When you have finished the first layer of the landform, check it for accuracy. Do this by placing the lid on top of the box. Looking down through the lid, compare the landform with the corresponding contour lines on the map, as shown in Figure 2. Remove, add, or reshape the modeling clay, if necessary.

8. Repeat Steps 6 and 7 for each layer of the landform until all of the contour lines of the map have a corresponding layer on the landform.

9. After you have finished your model, use the following questions to record your observations.

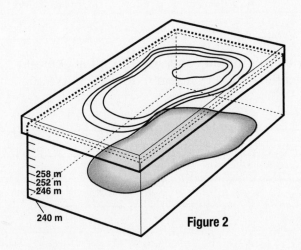

258 m
252 m
246 m

240 m

Figure 2

Name _____ Class _____ Date _____

Observations

1. What is the contour interval of the topographic map you used to make the landform?

_____

_____

_____

_____

2. Describe the shape of the landform you constructed.

_____

_____

_____

_____

3. How many meters above sea level is the base of your landform? How many meters above sea level is the top of your landform?

_____

_____

_____

_____

_____

Analysis and Conclusions

1. Using Models What does your landform indicate about the region modeled?

_____

_____

_____

2. Drawing Conclusions What might you conclude about the overall Earth processes that shaped the region that you modeled? Explain your answer.

_____

_____

_____

_____

_____

3. **Interpreting Diagrams/Photographs** Look at the topographic maps in Figure 3 on the next page. How does the topography of the Southwest map differ from the topographic features depicted in the other maps?

_____

_____

_____

_____

_____

4. **Comparing and Contrasting** Compare and contrast the topographic maps of the Southeast and the Southwest shown in Figure 3. Compare the processes that formed each landscape.

_____

_____

_____

_____

_____

5. **Inferring** Why do you think the landscape varies so much throughout the United States?

_____

_____

_____

_____

Go Further

Repeat the investigation using one of the two other maps shown in Figure 3 on the next page. Or obtain a topographic map of a small region in your state and make a three-dimensional landform of the region. Be sure to choose a region that does not cover too large an area and does not have too great a change in elevation so that your landform will still be reasonably accurate. Before you attempt this activity, show your map to your teacher. When your teacher approves your map, carry out the investigation. When you have completed the model, record your observations.

Southwest—Grand Canyon, Arizona
Contour interval: 50 meters

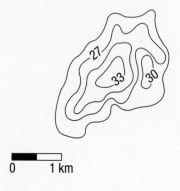

Northeast—Vermont
Contour interval: 30 meters

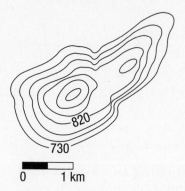

Southeast—Florida
Contour interval: 3 meters

Midwest—Wisconsin
Contour interval: 6 meters

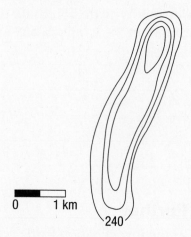

Figure 3 Some Hypothetical Topographic Maps from Different Parts of the United States

Crystal Systems

Introduction

Each of the more than 3800 minerals found on Earth has a distinct
crystal form that is the result of the mineral's internal arrangement of
atoms. These unique forms allow every mineral to be classified into one
of six crystal systems, which are shown in the Data Table. Crystals in
each system have a specific number of imaginary axes, which are
indicated by the letters *a*, *b*, and *c*. These axes can vary in length and
intersect at specific angles, designated by the Greek letters α, β, and γ.
The angles between adjacent faces of a crystal can be measured with a
simple instrument called a **contact goniometer.**

  In this investigation, you will make a contact goniometer and use it
to measure angles between adjacent faces of model crystals. You will
then use your measurements to identify the system to which each
model belongs.

Problem

How do crystal forms vary among
the six different crystal systems?

Pre-Lab Discussion

*Read the entire investigation. Then
work with a partner to answer the
following questions.*

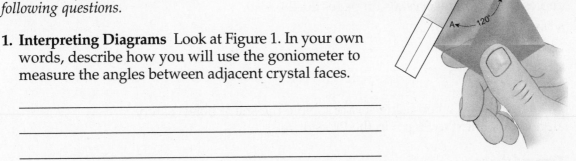

Figure 1

1. **Interpreting Diagrams** Look at Figure 1. In your own
   words, describe how you will use the goniometer to
   measure the angles between adjacent crystal faces.

   _____

   _____

   _____

   _____

2. **Comparing and Contrasting** Look at the Data Table. How are
   minerals in the orthorhombic and monoclinic systems the same?
   How do they differ?

   _____

   _____

   _____

   _____

3. **Comparing and Contrasting** Look at the Data Table. Compare and contrast characteristics of minerals in the cubic and triclinic systems.

_____

_____

_____

4. **Interpreting Diagrams** Study the diagrams in the Data Table. Which system of crystals has three identical planes of symmetry? Explain your choice.

_____

_____

_____

Materials *(per group)*

small, thin protractor (like the one shown in Figure 1)

stiff, white cardboard (~ 20 cm × 10 cm)

clear, quick-drying glue

metric ruler

thin, clear, rigid plastic strip (~ 15 cm × 2 cm)

hole punch

2 gummed reinforcements

metal brad

copies of the model crystals on pages 26–28

scissors

cellophane tape

Safety ✂

Always use care when using scissors. Note the sharp object safety alert symbol next to Step 5 in the Procedure.

Procedure
Part A: Constructing the Contact Goniometer

1. Use a thin layer of glue to bind the protractor to the cardboard. Make sure the base of the protractor is about 1 cm from and parallel to the bottom edge of the cardboard, as shown in Figure 1. Wait for the glue to dry completely before trying to use the instrument.

2. Use the hole punch to make a hole in the center of the plastic strip, as shown in Figure 1.

3. Use the hole punch to make a hole in the cardboard along the bottom edge, as shown in Figure 1. Moisten and place the gummed reinforcements over the hole on either side of the cardboard.

4. Use the metal brad to attach the plastic strip to the cardboard. Adjust the brad so that the plastic strip moves freely.

Name _____ Class _____ Date _____

Part B: Making and Measuring the Model Crystals

🔧 **5.** Carefully cut out each of the photocopied models provided by your teacher. Cut only along the outermost lines of each figure.

6. Using the Data Table as a guide, fold and tape the models to form six, three-dimensional crystals. After you make each fold, gently run your fingernail along the fold so that the angles between the faces in the model crystals will be more exact.

7. Use Figure 1 as a guide to measure the angles between adjacent faces in crystal A. Use your measurements to identify to which of the systems crystal A belongs. Record your choice on the appropriate line in the Data Table.

8. Repeat Step 7 for the other five model crystals.

Observations

DATA TABLE The Six Crystal Systems

System Name	Description	Typical Forms	
Cubic Model ____	All crystals in the cubic system have three axes that are all the same length. The axes intersect at 90° angles.	$a = b = c$; $\alpha = \beta = \gamma = 90°$	
Tetragonal Model ____	All crystals in the tetragonal system have three axes that intersect at 90° angles. Two of the axes are the same length.	$a = b \neq c$; $\alpha = \beta = \gamma = 90°$	
Hexagonal Model ____	All crystals in the hexagonal system have four axes. Three of the axes are the same length and intersect at 60° angles. The fourth axis is longer or shorter than the other three.	$a = b \neq c$; $\alpha = \beta = 90°$; $\gamma = 120°$	
Orthorhombic Model ____	All crystals in the orthorhombic system have three axes. Each axis is a different length. The axes intersect each other at 90° angles.	$a \neq b \neq c$; $\alpha = \beta = \gamma = 90°$	
Monoclinic Model ____	All crystals in the monoclinic system have three axes each of which is a different length. Two of the axes in these crystals intersect at a 90° angle. The third axis intersects the other two at an angle greater than 90°.	$a \neq b \neq c$; $\alpha = \beta = 90° \neq \gamma$	
Triclinic Model ____	All crystals in the triclinic system have three unequal axes that make oblique angles with each other.	$a \neq b \neq c$; $\alpha \neq \beta \neq \gamma \neq 90°$	

Model Crystals

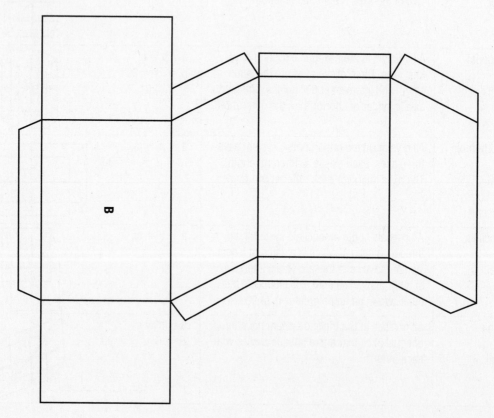

Name _____ Class _____ Date _____

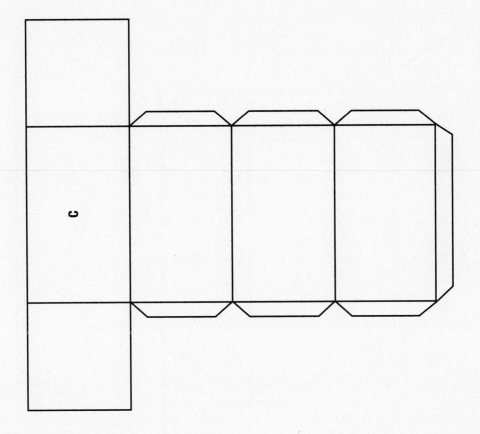

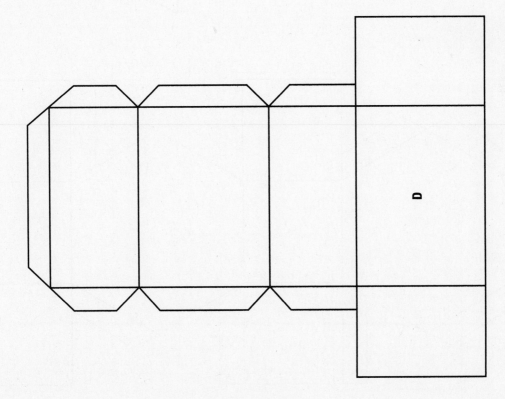

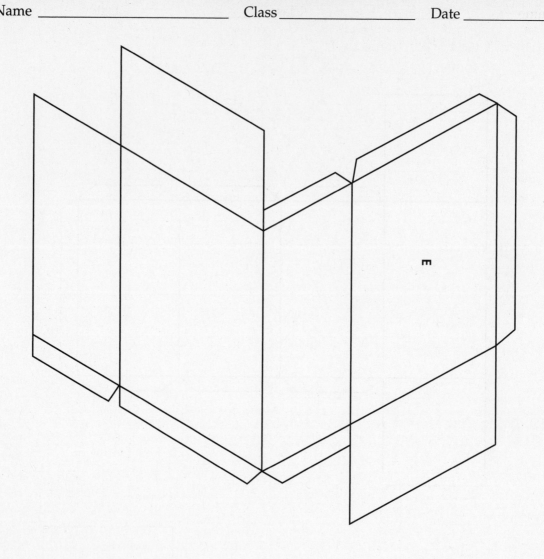

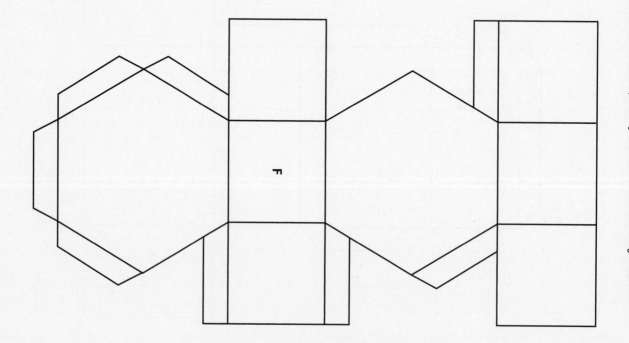

Analysis and Conclusions

1. **Classifying** To which crystal system does each of the models belong?

_____

_____

_____

_____

_____

2. **Comparing and Contrasting** How do the angles between major crystal faces differ among the various systems?

_____

_____

_____

_____

_____

3. **Drawing Conclusions** Why is crystal form probably the most useful property to use when identifying unknown minerals?

_____

_____

_____

_____

_____

Go Further

Study the crystals shown in the photographs on Resource 2 in the DataBank. Use what you've learned in this investigation to identify the crystal system to which each mineral belongs.

Classifying Rocks Using a Key

Introduction

Recall that a **rock** is a naturally occurring, solid mass of minerals or mineral-like matter. Geologists classify rocks into three major groups based on how the rocks form. **Igneous rocks** form when molten material—**lava** or **magma**—cools either on Earth's surface or underground. **Extrusive rocks** form when lava cools quickly at or near Earth's surface. Extrusive rocks have either a fine-grained texture or a glassy texture. **Intrusive rocks** form as magma cools slowly farther beneath Earth's surface. This slow rate of cooling allows mineral grains to grow large, and such a rock is said to have a coarse-grained texture.

Sedimentary rocks form when pieces of rocks, minerals, or organic matter—all of which are called **sediment**—are compacted and cemented. **Clastic rocks** are sedimentary rocks that are made of fragments of weathered Earth materials. The fragments might be fairly large, such as pebbles; somewhat smaller, such as grains of sand; or very small, such as grains of clay. **Chemical rocks** are sedimentary rocks that form when minerals settle out of solution. **Biochemical rocks** are sedimentary rocks that form as the result of organic processes.

Metamorphic rocks are rocks that form when existing rocks are subjected to changes in pressure or temperature. They can also form when they are subjected to chemical solutions. Metamorphic rocks may be **foliated,** which means that the components are arranged in parallel bands, or **nonfoliated,** which means that the rock's components are not arranged in bands.

In this investigation, you will observe rock **texture,** which is the shape, size, and arrangement of a rock's components. You will use rock texture and other properties to classify rocks using a key.

Problem

How can you use a key to classify rocks?

Pre-Lab Discussion

Read the entire investigation. Then work with a partner to answer the following questions.

1. **Inferring** What is the purpose of this investigation?

   _____

   _____

2. **Forming Operational Definitions** In your own words, describe what is meant by a rock's *texture.*

   _____

   _____

3. Observing What distinguishes the two main types of igneous rocks? Explain your answer.

_____

_____

_____

4. Drawing Conclusions Chalk is made of tiny fragments of marine organisms. To which group of rocks does chalk belong?

_____

_____

_____

5. Classifying Suppose you observe a rock with distinct bands. What type of rock might this be? Can the rock also belong to another group of rocks? Explain your answer.

_____

_____

_____

_____

_____

Materials (per group)

igneous rocks

sedimentary rocks

metamorphic rocks

bottle of dilute (1*M*)
  hydrochloric acid (HCl)
  with dropper

hand lens

paper towels

red pen or pencil

Safety

Put on safety goggles, a lab apron, and plastic disposable gloves. Take care when using chemicals such as hydrochloric acid as they may irritate the skin or stain skin or clothing. Never touch or taste a chemical unless instructed to do so. Wash your hands thoroughly after completing this investigation. Note all safety alert symbols next to the steps in the Procedure and review the meaning of each symbol by referring to the symbol guide on page xiii.

Procedure

 1. Put on your safety goggles, disposable gloves, and lab apron.

 2. Choose one of the rock samples provided by your teacher. Observe its texture, color, crystal size, and composition with and without the hand lens.

3. Use the Key to Rock Classification (Data Table 1) to classify the sample. Begin by reading the first question. Answer *Yes* or *No* based on your observations.

4. After the words *Yes* and *No*, you will find directions to proceed to another question, or you will discover to which group of rocks your specimen belongs. If you find directions to proceed to another question, go to that question, answer it, and follow the directions.

5. Continue working through the key in this way until you come to a statement that allows you to classify your rock sample. To answer Question 8 in Data Table 1, put the rock on a paper towel and place a single drop of HCl on the rock. **CAUTION:** *Always wear safety goggles and disposable gloves when working with chemicals.*

6. In Data Table 2, record the route that you take through the key, using the numbers of the questions. For example, your route could be "1—4—5—extrusive igneous rock." In the last column of the table, write the name of the rock group to which each sample belongs.

7. When you have classified all of the samples, remove and dispose of your rubber gloves and thoroughly wash your hands with soap and water.

8. Compare your classifications with those provided by your teacher. If you made a mistake in classifying any of the samples, put the correct answer in red next to your answer.

DATA TABLE 1

Key to Rock Classification	
1. Does the rock contain visible connecting crystals?	*Yes:* Go to Question 2. *No:* Go to Question 4.
2. Are all of the crystals the same color and shape?	*Yes:* The rock is a nonfoliated metamorphic rock (possibly marble or quartzite). *No:* Go to Question 3.
3. Are all of the crystals in a mixed "salt-and-pepper"pattern?	*Yes:* The rock is an intrusive igneous rock (possibly granite or diorite). *No:* The rock is a foliated metamorphic rock (possibly schist or gneiss).
4. Does the rock contain many small holes or have a uniform dark color?	*Yes:* The rock is an extrusive igneous rock (possibly pumice or basalt). *No:* Go to Question 5.
5. Is the rock glassy (does it resemble broken glass)?	*Yes:* The rock is an extrusive igneous rock (obsidian). *No:* Go to Question 6.
6. Does the rock have flat, thin layers that can be broken apart?	*Yes:* The rock is a foliated metamorphic rock (slate). *No:* Go to Question 7.
7. Does the rock contain pebbles, sand, or smaller particles that are cemented together?	*Yes:* The rock is a clastic sedimentary rock (possibly conglomerate, sandstone, or shale). *No:* Go to Question 8.
8. Does the rock fizz when dilute HCl is dropped on it?	*Yes:* The rock is chemical or organic sedimentary rock (limestone or chalk). *No:* Ask your teacher for assistance.

Name _____ Class _____ Date _____

Observations

DATA TABLE 2

Letter of Sample	Route Taken	Group to Which Rock Belongs

Analysis and Conclusions

1. **Using Tables and Graphs** How difficult was it to use the key to classify your rock samples? What problems did you encounter?

   _____

   _____

   _____

   _____

2. **Evaluating and Revising** For each sample that you incorrectly classified, retrace the route you took through the key. Do you need to correct your route? If so, write the correct route. If your route was correct, explain why you may have incorrectly identified the sample.

   _____

   _____

   _____

   _____

3. **Making Generalizations** How useful was rock color in classifying the rock samples? Explain your answer.

_____

_____

_____

_____

_____

_____

4. **Making Generalizations** Describe the overall texture of each of the major groups of rocks—intrusive, extrusive, clastic, chemical, foliated, and nonfoliated.

_____

_____

_____

_____

_____

_____

_____

_____

_____

5. **Comparing and Contrasting** Which two of the rock samples were the easiest to classify? What properties made them easy to classify?

_____

_____

_____

_____

_____

6. **Comparing and Contrasting** Which two rock samples were the hardest to classify? Explain your answer.

_____

_____

_____

_____

_____

7. Designing Experiments How could you change the procedure of this investigation to produce better results?

_____

_____

_____

_____

_____

Go Further

Collect at least ten different rocks samples from the area around your home or school. Label each rock with the location where you found it. Use the Key to Rock Classification (Data Table 1) to classify each of the rocks you gathered. **NOTE:** Always obtain permission **before** collecting rocks on public or private property. Only collect rocks when you are with a responsible adult.

Recovering Oil

Introduction

When marine organisms die, they begin to decay and then become buried. Over millions of years, the decaying organisms undergo various physical and chemical changes, finally forming petroleum, or crude oil. The rock in which the petroleum forms is called the **source rock.** Over time, petroleum, along with natural gas, often moves from the source rock and collects in permeable rocks called **reservoir rocks.** Impermeable rocks, or **cap rocks,** such as shale prevent the oil and gas from moving further.

Petroleum in subsurface traps is often recovered by drilling a well into the reservoir. In some cases, the petroleum automatically rises as a result of changes in pressure in the reservoir. In other cases, however, pressure must be applied by methods that involve pumping water into the reservoir. This method allows the oil to be brought to the surface because petroleum is less dense than water and will float on top of it.

In this investigation, you will use various methods to recover the maximum amount of oil from a model well.

Problem

How does water affect the recovery of oil from a well?

Pre-Lab Discussion

Read the entire investigation. Then work with a partner to answer the following questions.

1. **Predicting** What do you predict will happen when you add water to the bottle after the first attempt to remove the oil has been made?

   _____

   _____

   _____

   _____

2. **Predicting** Do you expect more oil to be removed from the model well when hot water or cold water is added to the well? Explain your answer.

   _____

   _____

   _____

   _____

Name _____ Class _____ Date _____

3. **Applying Concepts** How does adding water to an oil well change the pressure within the petroleum reservoir?

_____

_____

_____

_____

4. **Inferring** Different substances can be used to bring oil to Earth's surface. Why do you think water is used most often to get oil to flow from a well?

_____

_____

_____

_____

5. **Controlling Variables** What is the independent variable in this investigation?

_____

_____

_____

_____

6. **Controlling Variables** What is the dependent variable in this investigation?

_____

_____

_____

_____

Materials *(per group)*
plastic bottle with spray pump
plastic tubing to fit the pump nozzle
pea-sized pebbles
2 graduated cylinders
200 mL vegetable or mineral oil
4 250-mL beakers
cold tap water
hot tap water
paper towels
clock or watch with second hand
soap to clean glassware

Name _____ Class _____ Date _____

3. **Applying Concepts** How does adding water to an oil well change the pressure within the petroleum reservoir?

_____

4. **Inferring** Different substances can be used to bring oil to Earth's surface. Why do you think water is used most often to get oil to flow from a well?

_____

5. **Controlling Variables** What is the independent variable in this investigation?

_____

6. **Controlling Variables** What is the dependent variable in this investigation?

_____

Materials *(per group)*
plastic bottle with spray pump
plastic tubing to fit the pump nozzle
pea-sized pebbles
2 graduated cylinders
200 mL vegetable or mineral oil
4 250-mL beakers
cold tap water
hot tap water
paper towels
clock or watch with second hand
soap to clean glassware

Earth Science Lab Manual ▪ **38**

Safety 🧪🥼🧤🔥🔬⚠️

Wear your safety goggles and a lab apron during this investigation. Take care when working with the hot water to avoid burns. Be careful to avoid breakage when working with glassware. Wipe up any water or oil spills immediately. Wash your hands thoroughly after completing this investigation. Note all safety alert symbols next to the steps in the Procedure and review the meaning of each symbol by referring to the symbol guide on page xiii.

Procedure

🥼🧪 **1.** Put on your safety goggles and a lab apron.

🧤 **2.** Put pebbles into the plastic bottle until the bottle is half full, as shown in Figure 1.

⚠️🧤 **3.** Use one of the graduated cylinders to measure 100 mL of vegetable oil or mineral oil. Pour the oil into the bottle. **CAUTION:** *Be careful to avoid breakage when working with glassware. Also be careful not to spill any oil onto your clothing. Immediately wipe up any spills.*

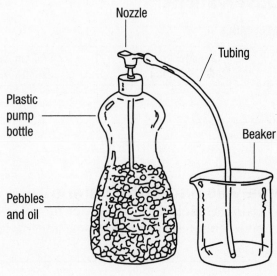

Figure 1

4. Place the spray pump onto the plastic bottle while gently working its tube down through the pebbles. Attach the plastic tubing to the nozzle. Place the other end of the tubing into a 250-mL beaker, as shown in Figure 1.

5. For 5 minutes, use the spray pump to remove as much oil as you can from the plastic bottle, which is your model well. Use the graduated cylinder to measure the amount of oil removed. Record this information in the Data Table.

6. Measure 80 mL of cold tap water in the second graduated cylinder. Add this water to the spray bottle. For 5 minutes, try to pump as much liquid as possible into a second beaker. Let the mixture stand for 1 or 2 minutes so that the oil and water separate. Carefully pour the oil layer that is on top of the water into the first graduated cylinder. In the Data Table, record the amount of oil you collected.

🔥 **7.** Rinse the bottle and pebbles with hot water to remove any excess oil. Dry them with paper towels. Place the used oil in the container designated by your teacher. Thoroughly clean the first graduated cylinder with soap and water. Add 100 mL of fresh oil. **CAUTION:** *Use extreme care when working with hot water to avoid burns.*

8. Repeat Steps 2 through 5. After Step 5, add 80 mL of hot tap water to the spray bottle. For 5 minutes, try to pump as much liquid as possible into a second beaker. Let the mixture stand for 1 or 2 minutes so that the oil and water separate. Carefully pour the oil layer that is on top of the water into the first graduated cylinder. In the Data Table, record the amount of oil you collected.

9. Place the used oil in the container designated by your teacher. The water with traces of oil can be poured down the sink. **CAUTION:** *Use extreme care when working with hot water to avoid burns.*

10. Wash your hands thoroughly after completing this investigation.

Observations

DATA TABLE

Oil Added to Model Well (mL)	Oil Removed Before Adding Water (mL)	Oil Removed After Adding Water (mL)
		cold water
		hot water

Analysis and Conclusions

1. Using Models How was your model reservoir like an actual petroleum reservoir? How was the model different?

_____

_____

2. Analyzing Data How did your results compare with your prediction?

_____

_____

_____

3. Observing Why were you unable to remove all the oil from the bottle when you pumped it in Step 5?

_____

4. Comparing and Contrasting How did adding cold water to the model oil well affect the amount of oil removed from the well? Hot water?

_____

_____

_____

_____

Desalinization by Distillation

Introduction

"Water, water everywhere, / Nor any drop to drink." This quotation is from *The Rime of the Ancient Mariner* by Samuel Taylor Coleridge, a poem that describes the fate of sailors in a boat that is stranded in the middle of the Pacific Ocean. The sailors are surrounded by water that they cannot drink. You might already know that both fresh water and seawater contain dissolved salts. But the amount of dissolved salts in a liter of seawater is much greater than the amount of dissolved salts in fresh water. Drinking seawater causes water to move out of cells in the body through a process called osmosis. This process can eventually cause dehydration and even death.

In regions where the supply of fresh water is limited, seawater can be treated to make it safe to drink. The general name for processes that remove salts from water is **desalinization.** One method for separating dissolved salts from water is called distillation. During the **distillation** process, a solution is heated until it vaporizes the liquid. The gaseous water is separated from the salt impurities. Then, as the vapor cools, the gas condenses to form liquid water that has been separated from the salts.

In Part A of this investigation, you will distill salt water by boiling it. In Part B of this investigation, you will use sunlight to vaporize the salt water.

Problem

How can you desalinize salt water?

Pre-Lab Discussion

Read the entire investigation. Then work with a partner to answer the following questions.

1. **Predicting** In Part A, how will the contents of the cooled flask differ from the contents of the heated flask?

   _____

   _____

   _____

2. **Inferring** In Part B, why is it important to keep the clear bottle away from direct sunlight?

   _____

   _____

   _____

   _____

3. **Formulating Hypotheses** In Part B, why is the bottle containing the salt water placed on a board? *Hint:* Assume that some water vapor condenses in the plastic tubing.

_____

_____

_____

_____

4. **Inferring** Why are you able to separate the table salt from the water in the salt water?

_____

_____

_____

_____

Materials *(per group)*

2 250-mL Erlenmeyer flasks

100-mL graduated cylinder

saltwater solution

aluminum foil (15 cm × 15 cm)

1 1-hole rubber stopper
  with glass tubing inserted

2 40-cm pieces of plastic tubing

2 pieces glass tubing,
  bent at right angles

500-mL beaker

crushed ice

matches

laboratory burner

ring stand and ring

wire gauze

heat-resistant gloves

2 2-L plastic bottles

duct tape

wooden board,
  at least 3 cm thick

glass-marking pen

2 100-mL graduated
  cylinders

Safety

Put on safety goggles and a lab apron. Be careful to avoid breakage when working with glassware. Never touch or taste any chemical unless instructed to do so. Use extreme care when working with heated equipment or materials to avoid burns. Be careful when using matches. Tie back loose hair and clothing when working with flames. Do not reach over an open flame. Note all safety alert symbols next to the steps in the Procedure and review the meaning of each symbol by referring to the symbol guide on page xiii.

Procedure
Part A: Distillation of Salt Water by Boiling

 1. Put on your safety goggles and a lab apron.

2. Use the graduated cylinder to measure 100 mL of the saltwater solution and pour it into the flask that will be heated.

3. Fill the beaker with crushed ice and position it away from the burner, as shown in Figure 1. Cover the second flask with aluminum foil, making sure that the glass tubing does not touch the bottom of the flask. Press the edges of the foil against the beaker. Place this flask in the crushed ice.

4. Connect the apparatus as shown in Figure 1.

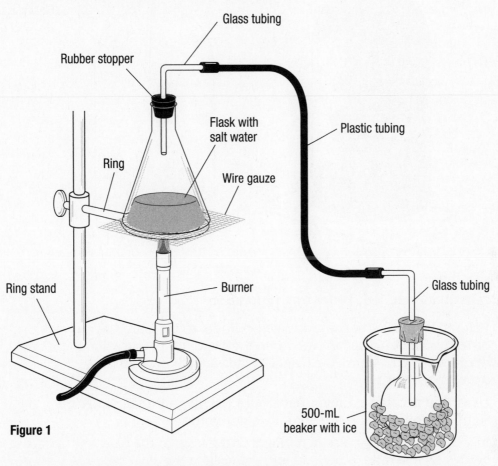

Glass tubing

Rubber stopper

Flask with salt water

Plastic tubing

Ring

Wire gauze

Ring stand

Burner

Glass tubing

500-mL beaker with ice

Figure 1

5. Using matches, carefully light the lab burner.

6. After about 8 to 10 minutes, carefully observe the flask in the beaker of crushed ice. **CAUTION:** *If necessary, carefully adjust the glass tubing so that it does not touch the liquid collecting in the flask.*

7. Continue collecting liquid in the cooled flask until about three-fourths of the liquid in the heated flask has been vaporized. Turn off the burner.

8. Observe the appearance of the contents of the cooled flask and the heated flask.

9. Put on heat-resistant gloves and remove the heated flask from the set-up. Allow the heated flask to cool. **CAUTION:** *Be careful handling equipment that has been heated. Hot glass looks like cold glass. Do not touch the heated flask or burner.*

10. Label and save the water in the cooled flask for the Go Further part of this investigation.

Name _____ Class _____ Date _____

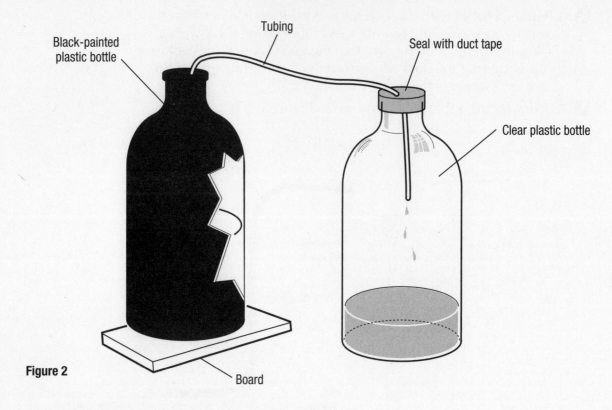

Tubing

Black-painted plastic bottle

Seal with duct tape

Clear plastic bottle

Figure 2

Board

Part B: Distillation of Salt Water by Evaporation

11. Refer to Figure 2. Use the graduated cylinder to measure 100 mL of tap water. Pour the tap water into the clear bottle. Use a glass-marking pencil to mark the height of the water. Now pour the water down the drain.

12. Use the graduated cylinder to measure 100 mL of the saltwater solution. Pour the solution into the black bottle.

13. Insert one end of the plastic tubing into the neck of the black bottle and insert the other end into the neck of the clear bottle.

14. While you and another student hold the two bottles in place, ask a third student to wrap the duct tape around the necks of the bottles so that the plastic tubing is held tightly in place.

15. With another student, move the setup to a windowsill that has exposure to sunlight during at least half of the day. Set the black bottle on the wooden board so that it is at a higher position than the clear bottle. Arrange the bottles so that the black bottle receives as much sunlight as possible and the clear bottle is kept out of the sun as much as possible.

16. Check the bottles daily until at least 75 percent of the liquid has been transferred to the clear bottle.

17. Disconnect the apparatus and observe the appearance of both liquids.

18. Pour the liquid from the clear bottle into the cooled flask from Part A. You will use this water in the Go Further part of this investigation.

Name _____ Class _____ Date _____

Analysis and Conclusions

1. **Comparing and Contrasting** What is the major difference between the experiments in Part A and Part B? What effect does this difference have on the experiments?

_____

_____

_____

_____

_____

2. **Observing** After you completed both parts of the investigation, how did the liquids in the heated flask and the black bottle differ from the liquids in the cooled flask and the clear bottle?

_____

_____

_____

_____

_____

3. **Applying Concepts** Suggest at least one procedure you could use to demonstrate that the liquids in the heated flask and black bottle and the cooled flask and clear bottle have different compositions.

_____

_____

_____

_____

_____

4. **Comparing and Contrasting** List the advantages of each method used in this investigation for distilling water. What are some disadvantages of each method?

_____

_____

_____

_____

_____

5. Applying Concepts Based on your results, which of these methods do you think would be most cost effective should distillation be used to provide more of our freshwater needs?

_____

_____

_____

_____

_____

6. Evaluating Even though desalinization of seawater is used along some coastlines today to provide fresh water, there are some disadvantages to this process. List at least three disadvantages of desalinization.

_____

_____

_____

_____

_____

Go Further 🔲

Without tasting the water, prove that the water in the cooled flask and the water in the clear bottle are fresh water. Pour 200 mL of salt water into a clean beaker. Pour 200 mL of the water you collected into another clean beaker. Predict what will happen if you place a fresh egg into each of the beakers. With your teacher's supervision, gently lower an egg into each beaker. Explain what you observe. Wash your hands thoroughly with soap or detergent after you complete the experiment.

Some Factors That Affect Soil Erosion

Introduction

Soil is a complex mixture of minerals, organic matter, air, and water. It is an integral part of Earth's lithosphere. Soil is home to billions of organisms, including many of the plants that people and other animals use as food. Soil stores nearly a quarter of Earth's fresh water, and it filters and decomposes many hazardous substances. Soil also plays an important role in Earth's cycles, including the nitrogen cycle and the carbon cycle.

You have learned that soil erosion depends on various factors including climate, slope, soil composition, and the type and amount of vegetation that grows in the soil. Some soil erosion is natural; however, much erosion is the result of human activities.

In this investigation, you will examine how slope affects soil erosion. You will also model some methods for reducing soil erosion.

Problem

How does slope affect soil erosion?

Pre-Lab Discussion

Read the entire investigation. Then work with a partner to answer the following questions.

1. **Posing Questions** Formulate a question that states the purpose of this investigation.

   _____

   _____

   _____

   _____

2. **Controlling Variables** What are the independent and dependent variables in this investigation?

   _____

   _____

   _____

   _____

3. **Inferring** Why will you add some water to the sand before doing this investigation?

_____

_____

_____

4. **Applying Concepts** What are some methods that can be used to reduce soil erosion on slopes?

_____

_____

_____

Materials *(per class)*

large aluminum pans (4 to 5 depending on class size)

heavy-duty trash bag

scissors

duct tape

protractor

play sand (25-lb bag)

plastic drinking straws (3 to 4 per group)

ruler

wooden blocks of various heights (2 to 3 per group)

1-L plastic bottle

sprinkling can

bucket or other containers to collect waste water

clock or watch

Safety 🜂 🚼 🜔 ✂ 🜍

Put on safety goggles and a lab apron. Be careful to avoid breakage when working with glassware. Also be careful when handling sharp instruments. Wash your hands thoroughly with soap and water after completing this investigation. Note all safety alert symbols next to the steps in the Procedure and review the meaning of each symbol by referring to the symbol guide on page xiii.

Procedure

Part A: Modeling Erosion

🜂🚼 1. Put on your safety goggles and a lab apron.

2. Pour sand into the aluminum pan and pack down the sand until there is a uniform layer of sand in the pan. The sand should be about 5 cm deep, as shown in Figure 1.

3. Lightly sprinkle a small amount of water over the sand to help pack down the sand.

4. Use one of the wooden blocks to prop up one end of the pan as shown.

5. Use the protractor to measure the angle the sand-filled pan has been raised by the wooden blocks. Record the angle for trial one in the Data Table.

6. Measure about 1000 mL of water into the sprinkling can. Slowly and evenly pour the water over the sand in the upper half of the pan.

7. Wait about 5 minutes for the erosion—movement of the sand—to stop. Observe how and where the sand erodes and how long it takes for the sand to begin eroding. Record your observations of the erosion.

8. Estimate the amount of sand (for example, one-third) that was eroded and deposited at the bottom end of the pan. Record the amount of sand eroded in the Data Table.

9. Scoop as much of the water out of the bottom end of the pan as possible and place the waste water in a bucket provided by your teacher. **CAUTION:** *Do not pour the sandy water down the drain.*

10. Repeat Steps 2 through 7 after placing more blocks under the pan or using a thicker block. Record your results for trial two in the Data Table.

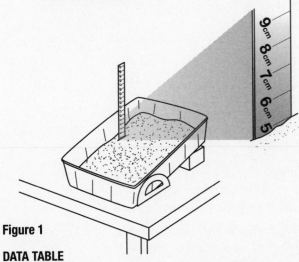

Figure 1

DATA TABLE

Trial	Angle of Pan	Amount of Sand Eroded	Observations
1			
2			
3			

Part B: Modeling Erosion Barriers

11. Remove as much of the water from the pan as possible, using the bucket provided by your teacher. **CAUTION:** *Do not pour the sandy water down the drain.*

12. Smooth and pack down the sand. Measure the angle of the pan. Record the angle of the pan in the Data Table.

13. Use the scissors to cut the trash bag into a 5-cm-wide strip that is long enough to extend across the width of the aluminum pan.

14. Cut 3 to 4 plastic drinking straws in half or in lengths of about 10 cm.

15. Place 5 to 6 plastic straw sections in a line that extends across the middle of the sand-filled pan. Push the straw sections as far down into the sand as possible. Space the straw sections evenly across the pan, with one straw placed close to each side of the pan.

16. Tape the trash bag strip onto the top of the straw sections that stick up out of the sand, as shown in Figure 2. This strip represents an erosion barrier.

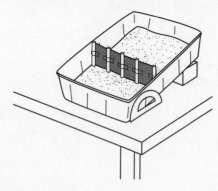

Figure 2

17. Measure about 1000 mL of water into the sprinkling can. Slowly and evenly pour the water over the sand in the upper half of the pan.

18. Wait about 5 minutes for the erosion to stop. Observe how and where the sand erodes and how long it takes for the sand to begin eroding. Record your observations of the erosion.

19. Estimate the amount of sand that was eroded and deposited in the bottom of the pan. Record the amount of sand that eroded for this trial.

20. Pour the sand and water into the bucket. **CAUTION:** *Do not pour sandy water down the drain.* Wash your hands thoroughly when you have finished the investigation.

Name _____ Class _____ Date _____

Analysis and Conclusions

1. **Comparing and Contrasting** In which trial of this investigation did the most soil erode?

   _____

   _____

   _____

   _____

2. **Relating Cause and Effect** Use your results to explain how slope affects the erosion of soil.

   _____

   _____

3. **Inferring** In the repeated trials of the investigation, what variable or condition changed? How did this affect the amount of erosion?

   _____

   _____

   _____

4. **Drawing Conclusions** How did the erosion barrier affect the amount of erosion?

   _____

   _____

   _____

5. **Applying Concepts** Where could erosion barriers like the one you constructed in the investigation be used to reduce or prevent erosion?

   _____

   _____

   _____

6. **Applying Concepts** How do you think soil erosion compares in dense forests, farms with crops planted in rows, and grasslands?

   _____

   _____

   _____

   _____

7. Controlling Variables How could you change the procedure in this investigation to obtain better results?

_____

_____

_____

_____

Go Further 🖳

Design a setup similar to the one used in the investigation that will explore the effect of different rates of rainfall. Pour water in the pan at faster and slower rates or in one location rather than over the entire pan and then compare the amount of erosion. Generate a detailed procedure and show it to your teacher. Once you have approval, predict what you think will happen and carry out the experiment. Dispose of the sand and water in a bucket provided by your teacher. Wash your hands thoroughly with soap or detergent after you complete the experiment.

Name _____ Class _____ Date _____

Chapter 6 Running Water and Groundwater   Investigation 6A

Rivers Shape the Land

Introduction

A **topographic map** is a model that represents Earth's three-dimensional surface in two dimensions. **Contour lines** on a topographic map connect points of equal elevation. The difference in elevation between adjacent contour lines is the **contour interval.** The vertical distance between the lowest and highest points shown on a topographic map is called **relief.** Closely spaced contour lines indicate a steep slope, while contour lines that are farther apart indicate a gentle slope. Like all maps, topographic maps have a **scale** that is used to show how horizontal distances on the map are related to actual distances shown on the map. Also like most other maps, topographic maps show a bird's-eye, or top, view of an area. Geologists often make **topographic profiles,** or side views, of an area to better visualize the change in elevation of an area.

The topographic map you will use in this investigation is of an area in Louisiana that is changed by the Red River and its tributaries. Like all streams, the Red River erodes materials from is channel and deposits these sediments elsewhere. Look at Resource 8 in the DataBank. Note that the width of the river's **floodplain,** or valley floor, in this part of Louisiana is shown by the solid line marked **A.** Other features shown on the map include levees, meanders, point bars, a yazoo tributary, an oxbow lake, and backswamps. A **natural levee** is a ridge made up mostly of coarse sediments that is parallel to a stream and forms when the stream overflows its banks. Sediment that accumulates on the inside of a **meander,** or curve in the stream, is a **point bar.** A **yazoo tributary** is a tributary that flows parallel to the main river on a floodplain. An **oxbow lake** is a branch of a stream that becomes cut off from the main stream. **Backswamps** are poorly drained areas on a river's floodplain.

In this investigation, you will use a topographic map to answer questions about the Red River. You will also make a topographic profile of a section of the map.

Problem

How does a river change the land over which it flows, and what do these features look like on a topographic map?

Pre-Lab Discussion

Read the entire investigation. Then work with a partner to answer the following questions.

1. **Interpreting Maps** What is the contour interval of this topographic map?

© Pearson Education, Inc., publishing as Pearson Prentice Hall. All rights reserved.

Earth Science Lab Manual ▪ **53**

2. Calculating Approximately how many inches on the map represent 5 miles on the surface?

_____

_____

3. Interpreting Maps In which part of the map is the topography rough with steeper slopes? Explain your answer.

_____

_____

_____

4. Interpreting Maps Find the hill labeled **A** in the southeastern corner of the map. What is the total relief between the Red River and the top of the hill?

_____

_____

5. Interpreting Maps In which direction do the three small bayous labeled **B** flow? How can you tell?

_____

_____

6. Inferring Recall that gradient is the slope or steepness of a stream channel. Describe the gradient of the Red River in this part of Louisiana. Explain.

_____

_____

Materials *(per group)*

pencil

metric ruler

plain white paper, 1 sheet

Resource 1 in the DataBank

Resource 8 in the DataBank

Procedure

1. To make a topographic profile, place the sheet of white paper along the vertical line marked **P-P′** in the eastern part of the map.

2. Mark each place where a contour line intersects the edge of the paper, as shown in Figure 1. Record the elevation of the contour line next to each mark on the paper. Note that in the southern portion of the map the contour lines are very closely spaced.

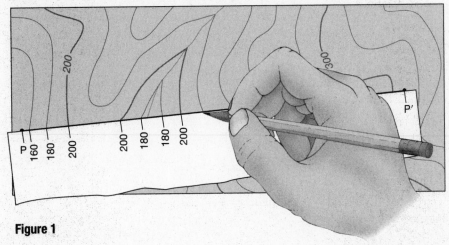

Figure 1

3. Based on the values you marked along the piece of paper, decide on a vertical scale for your profile. Include a value slightly lower than the lowest point recorded and a value slightly higher than the highest point recorded. Use the ruler to mark this scale on Figure 2. Adjust the horizontal scale of your profile so that it extends from P to P' on the graph below. Because the vertical scale is exaggerated, stretching the horizontal scale will produce a profile with more realistic looking slopes.

NORTH   SOUTH

P   P'

Figure 2   Your Topographic Profile

4. Lay your marked paper along the base of Figure 2. Wherever you have marked a contour line on the paper, place a dot directly above the mark at the appropriate elevation, as shown in Figure 3, the sample profile on the next page. **Note:** Values shown in Figure 3 are not the same as the values you marked on your paper.

5. Connect your points with a line. Again, note that your profile will not be the same as the one shown in Figure 3.

6. Label the floodplain area and the Red River on your topographic profile.

Name _____ Class _____ Date _____

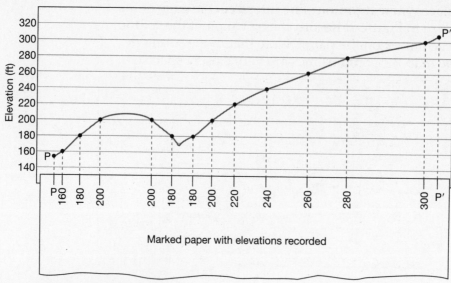

Figure 3   Sample Profile

Analysis and Conclusions

1. **Interpreting Maps** Describe your profile.

_____

_____

_____

_____

_____

2. **Calculating** Recall from your textbook that ultimate base level is
   sea level. Use your profile to determine approximately how many
   feet the Red River's floodplain is above ultimate base level.

_____

3. **Measuring** Use the topographic map to estimate the percentage of
   the map area that is the Red River's floodplain. Remember that the
   line on the map labeled **A** marks the width of the floodplain.

_____

4. **Predicting** Look at the lakes labeled G in relation to the course of
   the Red River. How might this part of the river change in the
   future? In your answer, include at least one piece of evidence from
   the map that supports your prediction.

_____

_____

_____

5. **Measuring** What is the approximate width of the river's floodplain, from the hills just north of Campti to the hills in the southern part of the map?

_____

6. **Interpreting Maps** Identify the structure on the map that is labeled **C**. How does such a structure form?

_____

_____

_____

_____

_____

_____

7. **Interpreting Maps** Identify the structure on the map that is labeled **D**. Explain how it formed.

_____

_____

_____

_____

_____

8. **Interpreting Maps** What kind of feature is labeled **E** on the topographic map? How might this feature have formed?

_____

_____

_____

9. **Interpreting Maps** What kind of feature is labeled **F** on the topographic map?

_____

_____

_____

Name _____ Class _____ Date _____

10. Modeling How would decreasing the contour interval to 10 feet affect your profile? How would increasing the contour interval to 40 feet affect your profile? Explain.

_____

_____

_____

_____

Go Further

Look again at the map. Write several sentences to explain how the Red River is changing its channel in this part of Louisiana and how the floodplain might change over the next 100 years.

Modeling Cavern Formation

Introduction

Caverns are chambers that form when acidic groundwater slowly erodes limestone formations beneath Earth's surface. These subsurface chambers, which are commonly called caves, form at or below the water table as groundwater flows along joints and bedding planes in the rocks. Many of the minerals dissolved by the groundwater are eventually deposited as dripstone features. **Stalactites** are icicle-like stone pendants that hang from the ceilings of most caverns. **Stalagmites** are features that form when a saturated water solution drops onto cavern floors and evaporates. This process leaves behind minerals that accumulate until they reach the cavern ceiling. Over time, a downward-growing stalactite and an upward-growing stalagmite might join to form a column.

In Part A of this investigation, you will model the formation of a cavern. In Part B, you will model how stalactites and stalagmites form.

Problem

How can you model the formation of caverns and their deposits?

Pre-Lab Discussion

Read the entire investigation. Then work with a partner to answer the following questions.

1. **Posing Questions** Write one question that summarizes the purpose of both parts of this investigation.

   _____

   _____

   _____

   _____

2. **Predicting** Based on the information given in the procedure for Part A, predict what you think will happen to the clay and its contents.

   _____

   _____

   _____

   _____

3. Using Models Why must the ball of clay used in Part A be below the surface of the water in the bowl?

_____

_____

_____

4. Forming Operational Definitions The solution that you will use in Part B of this investigation is a saturated solution. Use *only* the information given in Part B to describe in your own words what *saturated* means.

_____

_____

_____

_____

5. Inferring In Part B of this investigation, why will you place the string into one of the cups for several minutes before setting up the equipment?

_____

_____

_____

Materials *(per group of four students)*

~ 300 g modeling clay

5 small sugar crystals, cough drops, or hard candies

wooden skewer

medium-sized, clear, plastic bowl

hot tap water

250 mL white vinegar

large spoon

tongs

paper towels

serrated table knife

large graduated cylinder

large glass jar (1-L capacity)

800 mL Epsom salts, sugar, or table salt

60-cm cotton string

stirring rod

2 small metal washers

2 500-mL plastic drinking cups

all-purpose glue

piece of thick, corrugated cardboard (~ 20 cm × 40 cm)

Safety 🔲🔲🔲🔲🔲🔲

Put on safety goggles and a lab apron. Be careful to avoid breakage when working with glassware. Be careful when handling sharp instruments. Never taste any substance in the lab unless instructed to do so. Use extreme care when working with heated equipment or materials to avoid burns. Wash your hands thoroughly after completing this investigation. Note all safety symbols next to the steps in the Procedure and review the meanings of each symbol by referring to the symbol guide on page xiii.

Procedure

Part A: Modeling Erosion by Groundwater

1. Put on safety goggles and a lab apron.

2. Flatten the modeling clay to form a circle with a diameter of approximately 10 cm. Place the sugar crystals, cough drops, or hard candies along one edge of the circle so that each touches at least one other crystal, cough drop, or hard candy.

3. Shape the clay into a ball so that the crystals, cough drops, or hard candies are inside the ball. Place the ball of clay on your desk so that the solids are at the bottom of the ball.

4. Use the skewer to make at least five passageways that extend about three-fourths of the way into the ball of clay.

5. Place the bowl on your lab table or desktop. Fill the bowl halfway with hot tap water. Carefully add the vinegar to the water and stir the solution with the spoon.

6. Use the spoon to lower the clay ball into the bowl. If the clay is not completely covered with the water-vinegar solution, carefully add more hot water to the bowl until the clay is completely covered.

7. Allow the clay ball to stay in the solution for at least 30 minutes. Then proceed with Step 8. While you are waiting, start Part B of this investigation.

8. Layer two or three paper towels and fold them to form a square. Use the tongs to remove the clay from the solution and place it on the paper towels.

9. Use the serrated knife to cut the clay ball in half without squashing it. **CAUTION:** *Be careful when handling sharp instruments.*

10. In the space below, draw a cross-sectional, or side, view of the clay ball "cavern."

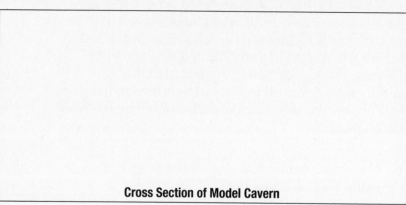

Cross Section of Model Cavern

Part B: Modeling Deposition by Groundwater

11. Use the graduated cylinder to measure and pour 650 mL of hot tap water into the large glass jar.

12. Add approximately half of the Epsom salts, sugar, or table salt to the water and stir until the crystals have completely dissolved.

13. Continue adding small amounts of the salts or sugar to the hot water until no more of the solid will dissolve.

14. Use the stirring rod to lower the string into the jar. Allow the string to soak in the solution for a few minutes.

15. Use the stirring rod to remove the string from the jar. Allow any excess solution to fall back into the beaker.

16. Tie a metal washer to each end of the string.

17. Place one end of the string into each cup, as shown in Figure 1. Allow some of the string to hang between the cups as shown.

18. With a partner, glue the cups onto the piece of cardboard as shown in Figure 1. Wait for the glue to dry then move the setup to a warm place where it will not be disturbed.

19. Use the graduated cylinder to measure and pour 300 mL of the saturated solution into each cup.

20. Wash your hands thoroughly after completing this investigation.

21. Observe your setup daily for about 2 weeks. If necessary, make and add more saturated solution to the cups.

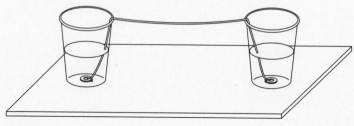

Figure 1

Analysis and Conclusions

1. **Using Models** What did the clay and crystals, cough drops, or hard candy represent in Part A of this investigation?

   _____

   _____

   _____

   _____

2. **Inferring** What was the purpose of adding vinegar to the hot water in Part A of this investigation?

   _____

   _____

   _____

3. **Relating Cause and Effect** Why did you make passageways into the ball of clay, and what do these features represent in the actual formation of caverns?

   _____

   _____

   _____

   _____

4. **Using Models** Explain why the ball of clay in Part A of this investigation had to be completely submerged in the water-vinegar solution.

   _____

   _____

   _____

5. **Designing Experiments** Why could the string in Part B of this investigation not touch the sides of the cups?

   _____

   _____

   _____

6. **Observing** In Part B of this investigation, which formed first—the stalagmites or stalactites? Explain why.

   _____

   _____

   _____

   _____

7. **Applying Concepts** Explain why dripstone features form after the formation of the cavern in which they are found.

_____

_____

_____

_____

8. **Designing Experiments** How might you alter your procedures for both parts of this investigation to get better results?

_____

_____

_____

_____

_____

Going Further

Once your dripstone features have completely hardened, carefully remove them from the string and cardboard and compare and contrast the shape and size of your stalagmites and stalactites.

Continental Glaciers Change Earth's Topography

Introduction

Glaciers are thick masses of ice that move slowly over the land. One type of glacier, **a continental glacier,** or ice sheet, is an enormous mass of ice that flows in all directions from one or more centers. Today, continental glaciers cover about 10 percent of Earth's landscape, where the climate is extremely cold. Thousands of years ago, however, these glaciers were more extensive than they are today. At one time, these thick sheets of ice covered all of Canada, portions of Alaska, and much of the northern United States. The impact that these ice sheets had on the landscape is still obvious today.

Landforms produced by continental ice sheets, especially those that covered portions of the United States, are mostly depositional in origin. Recall that there are two types of glacial deposits. **Stratified drift** is sediment that is sorted and deposited by glacial meltwater. **Till** is unsorted sediment deposited directly by a glacier. **Moraines** are ridges of till deposited as a glacier melts and recedes. **Ground moraines** are gently rolling plains of rocks and other glacial debris. Ground moraines can fill low spots and result in poorly drained swamplands. **End moraines** are deposits that form along the end of a melting glacier. An **outwash plain** is a ramp-like accumulation of sediment downstream from an end moraine. **Kettles** are glacial features that form when blocks of stagnant ice become buried and eventually melt. **Drumlins** are streamlined hills that are composed of till.

In this investigation, you will use a topographic map to examine some of the features produced by continental glaciation. Recall from Chapter 1 that a **topographic map** is a map that shows a bird's-eye, or top, view of an area. **Contour lines** on a topographic map connect points of equal elevation. The difference in elevation between adjacent contour lines is the **contour interval.** Closely spaced contour lines indicate a steep slope, while contour lines that are farther apart indicate a gentle slope. A **scale** shows how horizontal distances on the map are related to actual distances on Earth's surface.

Problem

How do continental glaciers change Earth's topography?

Pre-Lab Discussion

Read the entire investigation. Then work with a partner to answer the following questions.

1. **Measuring** What is the total length, in miles, of the glacial feature labeled **A**?

   _____

   _____

2. **Calculating** Approximately how long, in miles, is Blue Spring Lake? Show your calculations.

   _____

   _____

   _____

3. **Interpreting Diagrams/Photographs** How does the topography in the southeast corner of the map compare with the topography in the northwest part of the map?

   _____

   _____

   _____

4. **Interpreting Diagrams/Photographs** What features on the map indicate that portions of the area are poorly drained? Where are these features located?

   _____

   _____

   _____

5. **Comparing and Contrasting** How are glacial drift and till alike? How are they different?

   _____

   _____

   _____

Name _____ Class _____ Date _____

Materials *(per pair of students)*
metric ruler
Resource 1 in the DataBank
Resource 9 in the DataBank
calculator (optional)

Procedure

1. Closely examine the Whitewater, Wisconsin, topographic map (Resource 9 in the DataBank). If necessary, refer to the map symbol guide (Resource 1 in the DataBank).

2. Use the topographic map and what you have learned about glaciers to answer the **Analysis and Conclusions** questions.

Analysis and Conclusions

1. **Interpreting Diagrams/Photographs** The feature labeled **A** on the map is unsorted glacial debris. What is this structure, and how did it form?

_____

_____

_____

2. **Interpreting Diagrams/Photographs** What are the structures on the map labeled **B?** Find and label another example of this structure on the map.

_____

_____

_____

3. **Inferring** Where on the map is the likely location of the outwash plain?

_____

_____

4. **Interpreting Diagrams/Photographs** What are the structures on the map that are labeled **C?** How do these structures form?

_____

_____

_____

5. **Inferring** Where on the map might you find ground moraine?

_____

_____

Name _____ Class _____ Date _____

6. Applying Concepts In which direction did the continental glacier that changed this part of Wisconsin move? Give two lines of evidence to support your answer.

_____

_____

_____

_____

Go Further

If necessary, review how to make a topographic profile in Investigation 6A, Rivers Shape the Land. Then use the Whitewater topographic map to make a northwest-southeast topographic profile from the Scuppernong River to the city of Little Prairie.

Modeling Liquefaction

Introduction

When coffee is packed in a vacuum, the air is removed from the package. This vacuum packaging causes the coffee grounds to compact. When the package is opened, air moves among the coffee grounds and allows them to once again move freely within the package.

   Water trapped in sandy soil can cause the soil to behave like a liquid if external forces are applied faster than the water can escape the soil. The soil behaves like a liquid when water pressure is equal to the forces acting on the soil. This process is called **liquefaction.** Liquefaction often occurs when an earthquake strikes because the forces associated with the shaking and vibration at the surface of Earth cause sand particles to move away from one another. Because the grains are not in contact with one another, the soil loses strength and is said to liquefy.

   In this investigation, you will model sand liquefaction, a common phenomenon in certain earthquake-prone areas.

Problem

How can you model sand liquefaction?

Pre-Lab Discussion

Read the entire investigation. Then work with a partner to answer the following questions.

1. **Posing Questions** Write a question that summarizes the purpose of this investigation.

   _____

   _____

2. **Controlling Variables** What is the independent variable in this investigation?

   _____

   _____

3. **Controlling Variables** What is the dependent variable in this investigation?

   _____

   _____

4. Designing Experiments Why will you glue filter paper to the bottom of the rubber stopper?

_____

_____

5. Comparing and Contrasting How do you think the balloon holding dry sand will feel when you squeeze it? How will this compare with the balloon holding wet sand?

_____

_____

_____

_____

Materials *(per pair of students)*

large, round rubber balloon

large drinking straw

rubber stopper with hole for drinking straw

filter paper

scissors

all-purpose glue

funnel

500 g clean, dry, medium-grained sand

250-mL graduated cylinder

tap water

measuring cup

vacuum pump

Safety 🥽 🧤 ✂️ 🔥 ⚠️

Put on safety goggles. Be careful to avoid breakage when working with glassware. Be careful when handling sharp instruments. Observe proper laboratory procedures when using electrical equipment. Use the vacuum pump to remove most of the air from the balloon. Note all safety symbols next to the steps in the Procedure and review the meanings of each symbol by referring to the symbol guide on page xiii.

Procedure

🥽 1. Put on safety goggles.

2. Insert the straw into the hole in the rubber stopper so that the bottom edge of the straw is flush with the bottom of the stopper.

✂️ 3. Trace the circumference of the bottom of the stopper onto the filter paper. Cut out the circle and glue it to the bottom of the stopper. Wait for the glue to dry completely.

4. Work with a partner and use the funnel to fill the balloon halfway with sand.

5. Hold the balloon by the neck and gently squeeze the sand-filled portion with your fingers. Record your observations in the Data Table.

6. Pull the neck of the balloon over the bottom of the rubber stopper. Attach the tubing from the vacuum pump to the top of the straw and remove nearly all of the air from the balloon. Pinch the neck to close off the balloon.

7. Again, hold the balloon by the neck and gently squeeze the sand-filled portion with your fingers. Record your observations in the Data Table.

8. Remove the tubing from the straw and remove the balloon from the rubber stopper.

9. Use the graduated cylinder and funnel to add water to the sand-filled balloon. Add only enough water to make the sand wet. The amount of water you put into the balloon should be equal to about half of the amount of sand in the balloon.

10. Gently squeeze the balloon holding the sand-water mixture to wet the sand grains evenly.

11. Gently force excess air out of the balloon and tie the balloon at the bottom of the neck.

12. Gently squeeze the balloon and record your observations in the Data Table.

13. Gently but quickly squeeze the balloon five or six times. Record your observations in the Data Table.

Observations

DATA TABLE

Trial	Observations
Balloon with sand	
Balloon with sand (air removed)	
Balloon with sand and water (slow squeezing)	
Balloon with sand and water (rapid squeezing)	

Analysis and Conclusions

1. **Comparing and Contrasting** Compare and contrast the ease of movement of the dry sand in the balloon before and after air was removed from the balloon. Explain why this happened.

   _____

   _____

   _____

   _____

2. **Comparing and Contrasting** Compare and contrast the movement and feel of the wet sand when you squeezed slowly and when you squeezed rapidly.

   _____

   _____

3. **Inferring** What role does friction play in liquefaction?

   _____

   _____

4. **Using Models** What happens when water pressure increases in sandy soil in an earthquake-prone area?

   _____

   _____

5. **Applying Concepts** Study the observations you recorded in the Data Table. If you were to build a structure on one of these soils, which would you choose to prevent earthquake damage to the structure? Explain your choice.

   _____

   _____

6. **Designing Experiments** How could you redesign this investigation to produce better results?

   _____

   _____

   _____

   _____

Name _____ Class _____ Date _____

Design and Build a Simple Seismograph

Introduction

A **seismograph** is an instrument that records movements of the ground caused by earthquakes, explosions, and other ground-shaking events. All seismographs have a weight, a support that is anchored to the ground, and a device that records the vibrations.

When earthquake waves reach a seismograph, the inertia of the suspended weight keeps it stationary while the support vibrates with the ground motion. Some seismographs record vertical motions. The weight on such an instrument is often suspended from a metal spring, and the movements are recorded on a vertical drum.

Other seismographs record horizontal movements of the ground. These instruments use a weight suspended from a wire to sense and record vibrations on a horizontal drum. A record of any ground movements is called a **seismogram.**

In this investigation, you will design, build, and test a simple seismograph to record movements. You will also evaluate the seismograms produced by your instrument.

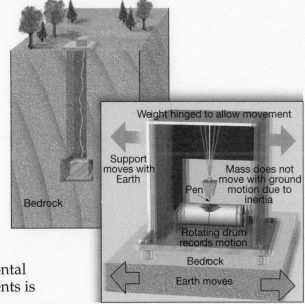

Figure 1 How a Seismograph Works
The inertia of the suspended mass tends to keep it motionless, while the recording drum, which is anchored to bedrock, vibrates in response to seismic waves.

Problem

How can you build and test an instrument that will record ground vibrations?

Pre-Lab Discussion

Read the entire investigation. Then work with at least three other students to answer the following questions.

1. Relating Cause and Effect Explain how a seismograph works.

_____

_____

_____

_____

2. **Inferring** Look again at the suggested materials list. Why do you think one of the suggested materials is a small brick?

_____

_____

3. **Using Models** Why do you have to make sure that the roll of adding machine paper is able to turn?

_____

_____

_____

4. **Relating Cause and Effect** How will your group produce "earthquakes" of various magnitudes?

_____

_____

Suggested Materials (per group of four or five students)

thin (~2.5 cm thick) wood planks	duct tape	small (~30–40 cm long) wood beams
heavy cord or wire	hammer	vice grips
hand saws	sharp pencil with soft lead	nails and screws
wire cutters	wood dowels	metric ruler
hand drills	adding machine tape	small, thin brick

Note: Ask your teacher for any other materials that you think might be useful to build your seismograph.

Safety 🥽 🔪 ⚠

Wear your safety goggles during this entire investigation. Use care when handling sharp instruments. Observe proper safety procedures when using the hammer, saws, and drills. Be careful when handling the wood to avoid getting splinters in your skin. Note all safety symbols next to the steps in the Procedure and review the meanings of each symbol by referring to the symbol guide on page xiii.

Design Your Own Investigation

🥽 1. Put on your safety goggles.

2. Reread the **Introduction** and the list of **Suggested Materials.** Also refer to Figure 1, which illustrates how a seismograph works, and Figures 2 and 3, which show examples of built seismographs. Use this information to draw and label a sketch of your proposed seismograph in the space provided on page 76. Make any necessary notes on your design.

3. On page 77, write the steps you will take to build your seismograph. Add as many steps as you need. Be sure to include any additional materials you may need.

✂️ ⚠️ 4. Have your teacher approve your design and procedure. Work with at least three other students to construct your seismograph. **CAUTION:** *Use care when using saws and drills. Also take care when using the hammer and sharp instruments.*

5. When your instrument is complete, test it to make sure that it records vibrations. If necessary, determine how to change your instrument so that it works properly. Discuss your proposed changes with your teacher and have your teacher approve the changes. Make the necessary changes and test your seismograph again. Continue to make changes as necessary.

6. Once your seismograph is working properly, anchor it to a tabletop with vise grips. Then simulate an earthquake 10 times. Each "earthquake" should be of various magnitudes. Be sure that the paper is being pulled at a regular rate as the simulated quake strikes. Label each of the seismograms accordingly.

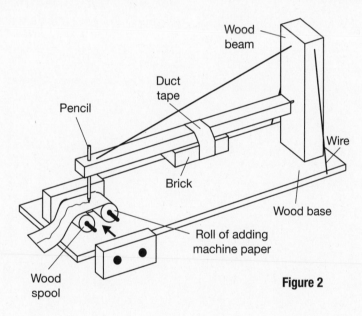

Figure 2

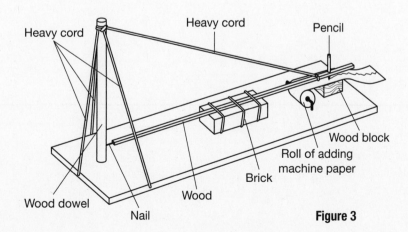

Figure 3

Name _____ Class _____ Date _____

Labeled Sketch of Proposed Seismograph

Name _____ Class _____ Date _____

Procedure

Step 1: _____

_____

_____

_____

_____

Step 2: _____

_____

_____

_____

_____

_____

Step 3: _____

_____

_____

_____

_____

_____

Step 4: _____

_____

_____

_____

_____

_____

Step 5: _____

_____

_____

_____

_____

_____

Step 6: _____

_____

_____

_____

_____

_____

Name _____ Class _____ Date _____

Analysis and Conclusions

1. **Observing** What type of movement—horizontal or vertical—were you able to record with your seismograph?

_____

_____

_____

2. **Using Models** What is the purpose of the brick?

_____

_____

_____

3. **Using Models** Why did you anchor the seismograph to a tabletop before simulating the earthquakes?

_____

_____

_____

_____

4. **Comparing and Contrasting** How did the seismograms produced during each "earthquake" compare? How were they different?

_____

_____

_____

5. **Designing Experiments** How could you redesign this investigation to produce better results?

_____

_____

_____

Go Further

Draw and label a seismograph that could be built to measure vertical movements.

Modeling a Plate Boundary

Introduction

The lithosphere is divided into moving segments called **plates.** The plates move as units relative to all other plates. All major interactions occur among individual plates along boundaries. Scientists first attempted to outline the plate boundaries by using locations of earthquakes. Later research showed plates bounded by three distinct types of boundaries, which exhibit different types of movement.

A **convergent boundary** is formed when two plates slowly move together. At this boundary, the leading edge of one plate is bent downward, sliding beneath the second plate. This process is called subduction, and the convergent boundaries are called **subduction zones.** The surface expression produced by one plate sliding below another plate is an **ocean trench.**

Just south of the Aleutian Islands in the northern Pacific Ocean, the Pacific plate moves northward and is subducted beneath the North American plate. A large number of earthquakes occur in this region. In this investigation, you will use earthquake data from one part of this region to form a model of the convergent boundary between the two plates.

Problem

How can you use earthquake data to model a convergent boundary between two plates?

Pre-Lab Discussion

Read the entire investigation. Then work with a partner to answer the following questions.

1. **Posing Questions** Write a question that summarizes the purpose of this investigation.

   _____

   _____

   _____

2. **Controlling Variables** What is the dependent variable in this investigation?

   _____

   _____

   _____

3. Controlling Variables What is the independent variable in this investigation?

_____

_____

_____

4. Inferring Why should the graph of earthquake depth vs. earthquake latitude have a zero at the top of the vertical axis?

_____

_____

_____

5. Predicting How do you think earthquake depth is related to the distance from an ocean trench?

_____

_____

_____

Materials *(per pair of students)*
ruler

protractor

Resource 3 in the DataBank

Procedure
1. Examine the map on Resource 3 in the DataBank. Study the convergence of the Pacific plate and the North American plate just south of the Aleutian Arc of volcanic islands in the northern Pacific Ocean.

2. Draw and label a diagram showing how the edges of the Pacific plate and the North American plate converge. Use Figure 1 to help you draw this diagram.

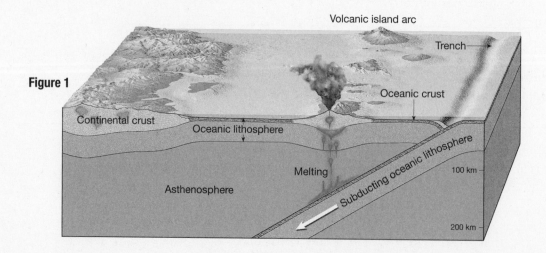

Figure 1

Name _____ Class _____ Date _____

3. The Data Table below shows the depths of foci and latitudes of earthquakes in the Aleutian Islands. All of the earthquakes in the table occurred near 180°W longitude. Examine the table of earthquake data and record any patterns you observe.

_____

_____

_____

DATA TABLE

Earthquake	Year	Latitude of Epicenter (°N)	Depth of Focus (km)
1	1982	51.39	51
2	1983	51.97	116
3	1984	51.13	15
4	1985	52.36	213
5	1985	52.62	233
6	1986	51.70	67
7	1986	52.31	170
8	1987	51.29	22
9	1987	51.93	94
10	1990	52.30	143
11	1991	51.96	108
12	1992	52.01	99
13	1992	52.13	130
14	1992	52.48	211
15	1995	51.19	29
16	1997	51.28	33
17	1998	51.59	43
18	1999	51.87	72
19	2000	51.60	71
20	2001	51.32	55
21	2001	51.77	79
22	2003	51.15	11
23	2003	52.13	180

4. Use the information in the Data Table to construct a graph showing the location and depth of the earthquakes. Use the following grid and plot the latitude on the horizontal axis and the depth of the focus on the vertical axis. Number the vertical axis with zero at the top and maximum depth at the bottom. Give your graph an appropriate title.

5. After plotting the data, draw a straight line that comes as close as possible to each of the data points.

Name _____ Class_____ Date _____

Title: _____

Degrees North Latitude

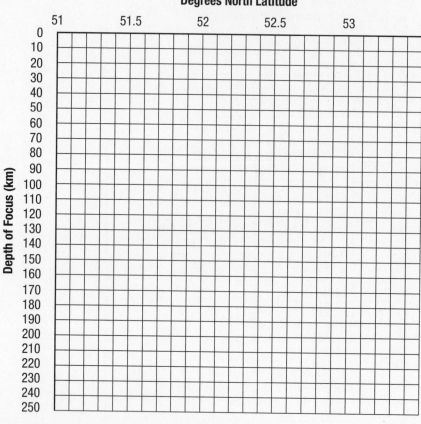

Analysis and Conclusions

1. Using Graphs What relationship exists between the depths of the earthquake foci and the latitude?

_____

_____

2. Analyzing Data How does the graph illustrate that the boundary between the Pacific plate and the North American plate is a convergent boundary?

_____

_____

_____

3. Applying Concepts The Aleutian trench is located where the two plates meet at the surface of the lithosphere. Use the graph to determine the approximate latitude of the Aleutian trench at 180°W longitude. Explain your answer.

_____

_____

_____

Name _____ Class _____ Date _____

4. **Using Graphs** Use the slope of the graph to determine how quickly the convergent boundary descends as latitude increases.

_____

_____

_____

5. **Calculating** A change in latitude of one degree corresponds to a distance of approximately 111 km along a north–south line. Using this information and your answer to Question 4, determine how far the convergent boundary descends as it moves 1 km northward. Show your work.

Use your results from Question 5 to help you answer Questions 6 and 7.

6. **Using Models** Draw a triangle that shows a side view of the convergent boundary with the correct scale relationship between horizontal distance and depth. Measure the angle at which the subducted plate descends beneath the upper plate. This is called the subduction angle.

7. **Calculating** Imagine there is a volcanic island arc on the surface of the lithosphere above the area where the descending plate reaches a depth of 100 km. Approximately how far north of the trench are the islands located? Show your work.

8. **Evaluating and Revising** Are all of the data points you plotted on the graph close to the straight line you drew to best fit the data? Provide possible explanations for your answer.

_____

_____

_____

_____

9. **Applying Concepts** Is the year in which an earthquake occurred an important variable in this investigation? Explain.

_____

_____

_____

_____

Go Further

The United States Geological Survey provides earthquake data from locations around the world. Obtain earthquake data near a divergent boundary such as an oceanic ridge or a transform fault boundary such as the San Andreas Fault. Graph some data points to see whether the depths of the foci of the earthquakes change as the distance from the boundary increases. Compare your findings to the results from this investigation. Explain any differences.

Interpreting a Geologic Map

Introduction

Geologic maps show the distribution of rock units at Earth's surface, as if the soil and other loose material had been stripped away. The rock is divided into units called **formations** that can be recognized and traced across the map area. Formations are identified by a color and/or pattern. Each unit is labeled with a letter abbreviation that indicates the age and name of the unit. The boundaries between formations are indicated by solid lines called **contacts.** If the boundary is uncertain or difficult to accurately locate, the contact will be shown as a dashed line. Geologic maps also show features such as **faults, folds,** and **unconformities,** as well as contour lines that indicate the elevations of the formations.

In this investigation, you will identify and interpret features on a geologic map for a portion of the northern Rocky Mountains.

Problem

What information can be obtained from a geologic map?

Pre-Lab Discussion

Read the entire investigation. Then work with a partner to answer the following questions.

1. **Posing Questions** Write a question that summarizes the purpose of this investigation.

   _____

   _____

   _____

2. **Interpreting Diagrams** What do the lightly colored lines that are labeled with numbers represent?

   _____

   _____

   _____

3. **Observing** How can you determine the age of the rock units shown on the map?

   _____

   _____

   _____

Name _____ Class _____ Date _____

Materials *(per group of students)*
Resource 6 in the DataBank
Resource 7 in the DataBank
map of North America or atlas
colored pencils
string
ruler
protractor

Procedure

1. Carefully study the geologic map, Resource 6. Match rock units, shown on the map as areas of different colors and patterns, with the descriptions of those units on the map key.

2. The square grids on the topographic base map represent numbered sections in a Township and Range grid system. The grids can be used to help locate features on the map. Determine the state, counties, latitude and longitude of the geologic map using the map, map key, and a map of North America or an atlas.

_____

_____

3. To measure distances on the map that are not on a straight line, use a string to follow the outline of the feature. Curve the string along the feature, holding one end of the string where you want to begin the measurement. Hold the string at the end of the feature. Be sure to continue holding the string at the starting point and ending point. Straighten out the string along the bar scale on the map or along the ruler to determine the measurement of the feature.

4. Maps provide a two-dimensional picture of the geology. In order to examine the geology in the third dimension, a cross section or profile is needed. To construct a cross section, first determine the line of section. A line of section XX' has been provided on the map. First, take a piece of paper and lay it on the map along line XX'.

5. Make small marks on the paper where a geologic contact or fault crosses the line of section. Transfer these contacts to the graph where you will construct your cross section.

6. Examine the map to determine what formations are present in your cross section. Label the formations on your cross section.

7. To determine the orientation of the geologic contacts, examine the map for strike-and-dip symbols. These are small T-shaped symbols with a number next to the short end of the *T*. This number represents the angle the rock units make with a horizontal line. This angle is called the **dip** of the unit. Locate any strike-and-dip symbols near the line of section.

8. Using the protractor, draw the contacts on your cross section with the correct angles.

9. On your cross section, draw all the contacts as straight lines from the angle. Label all the formations using the labels on the map key in the DataBank.

10. Make a cross-section key using the same labels and colors found on the map key in the DataBank. Use colored pencils to complete your cross section.

X   X′

Cross Section XX′

Analysis and Conclusions

1. **Observing** What is the scale of the map?

_____

2. **Measuring** What is the length of the stream on the west side of the map from the north edge of section 10 to the west edge of section 15?

_____

3. **Observing** What is the contour interval on the map?

_____

4. **Observing** In what direction does the stream in Question 2 flow? Explain how you can determine the direction of flow.

_____

_____

_____

5. **Calculating** What is the gradient of the stream from the north edge of section 10 to the west edge of section 15? **NOTE:** Gradient is the change in elevation divided by the change in distance.

6. Analyzing Data What geologic structure is exposed on the eastern half of the map? Explain.

_____

_____

_____

7. Interpreting Diagrams What is the oldest rock unit that is exposed on the map?

_____

_____

8. Interpreting Diagrams What age is the rock unit labeled *ad* in the southeast corner of the map? What type of rock makes up this unit?

_____

_____

9. Drawing Conclusions If you walk across a fault from the side where the Flathead quartzite is exposed to the side where the Empire shale is exposed, which side of the fault has moved up? Explain how you can determine which side of the fault moved.

_____

_____

_____

_____

_____

_____

_____

_____

Go Further

Construct a cross section that extends across the entire map by extending the XX' line of section to the western edge of the map. What structure is exposed in the northwest corner of the map?

Modeling Radioactive Decay

Introduction

When scientists learned to measure radioactive decay, they gained the ability to determine the ages of many rocks, minerals, fossils, and archaeological objects. **Radiometric dating** is the name of the procedure that scientists use for these age determinations. It relies on the constant rate of radioactive decay that occurs among radioactive isotopes such as uranium-238, thorium-232, potassium-40, and carbon-14. This rate is expressed as a **half-life,** which is the amount of time it takes for one-half of the nuclei in a sample of a radioactive isotope to decay into the stable daughter product.

In this investigation, you will model radioactive decay using pennies and then use your results to practice the radiometric dating procedure.

Problem

How can you model radioactive decay using pennies?

Pre-Lab Discussion

Read the entire investigation. Then work with a partner to answer the following questions.

1. **Using Models** What is the advantage of creating a simple model of radioactive decay?

   _____

   _____

   _____

   _____

2. **Inferring** Why is a penny useful for representing a radioactive isotope?

   _____

   _____

   _____

3. **Using Models** What represents the parent atoms in this activity? What represents the daughter atoms?

   _____

   _____

   _____

   _____

4. Predicting How will the abundance of the heads-up and tails-up pennies change over time during this activity?

_____

_____

_____

5. Contrasting Identify three ways in which this model differs from the actual process of radioactive decay.

_____

_____

_____

Materials *(per pair of students)*

flat box with a lid, such as a shoebox
100 pennies

Procedure

1. Place 100 pennies heads-up in the bottom of the box.
2. Cover the box with its lid and shake the box vigorously.
3. Set the box down and open it. Remove all pennies that are tails up. Count the remaining pennies and record the number in the Data Table below.
4. Cover the box containing the remaining heads-up pennies. Shake the box vigorously.
5. Repeat Steps 3 and 4 until no pennies remain in the box.

Observations

DATA TABLE

Shake #	Number of Heads-Up Pennies in Box
0	
1	
2	
3	
4	
5	
6	
7	
8	
9	
10	

Name _____ Class _____ Date _____

GRAPH

Construct a line graph of your data on the grid below. On the horizontal axis, plot the "shake number." On the vertical axis, plot the "number of pennies in box." Connect the points with a line. Give your graph an appropriate title.

Title: _____

Analysis and Conclusions

1. **Observing** What percentage of the original 100 pennies remained after the first shake of the box? The second shake? The third shake? What fractions do these percentages represent?

   _____

   _____

   _____

2. **Inferring** How are the above fractions related to the probability of each penny landing heads-up?

   _____

   _____

   _____

3. **Inferring** In terms of radioactive decay, what did each shake of the box represent?

   _____

4. **Inferring** In terms of radioactive decay, what did the number of remaining pennies in the box after each shake represent?

   _____

   _____

6. **Applying Concepts** After four shakes of the box, what is the parent/daughter ratio?

   _____

7. **Applying Concepts** Suppose the radioactive isotope you are modeling has a half-life of 713 million years. How old is the sample if 1/32 of the original isotope remains?

   _____

8. **Applying Concepts** Some fossil bones contain 1/8 of their original amount of carbon-14. How many half-lives have passed? How old are the bones?

   _____

Go Further

Use research resources in the library or on the Internet to find at least one instance where geologists or archaeologists used radiometric dating in their work. Write a paragraph describing what they determined, which radioactive isotope was used for the dating procedure, and why it was important to determine the age of the object(s) they measured.

Determining Geologic Ages

Introduction

Evidence of past life on Earth can be found in the fossil record. **Fossils** are among the most important tools scientists use to interpret Earth's history. Not only can they help in dating rock layers, they also reveal the changing nature of life over the vast scale of Earth's history. Fossils and **relative** and **absolute dating** have also told us what we know about geologic changes on Earth—from the gradual rearrangements of the continents to cataclysms that caused mass extinctions.

In this investigation, you will try your hand at using fossils, relative dating, and radiometric dating to uncover some of Earth's history.

Problem

How can you interpret the fossil record to determine Earth's history?

Pre-Lab Discussion

Read the entire investigation. Then work with a partner to answer the following questions.

1. **Inferring** This activity incorporates information from Chapters 12 and 13. How are these two chapters related?

   _____

   _____

   _____

   _____

2. **Inferring** Why is it important to have more than one dating technique available?

   _____

   _____

   _____

3. **Using Analogies** Look at the Geologic Time Scale (Resource 10) in the DataBank. How are eras, periods, and epochs like the divisions used in textbooks?

   _____

   _____

   _____

Name _____ Class _____ Date _____

4. Posing Questions Write a question that summarizes the purpose
of this activity.

_____

_____

_____

Materials *(per pair of students)*
geologic block diagram (Figure 1)
logarithmic scale showing decay of U-235
Resource 10 in the DataBank
Resource 11 in the DataBank

Procedure

Part A: Understanding Relative Dating

1. Carefully study Figure 1, the geologic block diagram below. Use the
   rules you have learned for determining relative age to find the
   sequence of geologic events. List their letters from oldest to
   youngest in the space provided beside the figure.

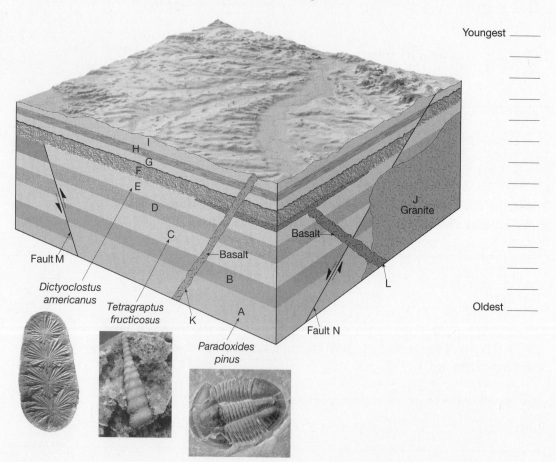

Youngest _____
_____
_____
_____
_____
_____
_____
_____
_____
_____
_____
_____
Oldest _____

Figure 1

Part B: Understanding Half-Life

2. Study Data Table 1 below. It contains information about the parent-daughter ratios of the isotope uranium-235 (U-235) for several of the rock layers in the block diagram.

DATA TABLE 1

Parent-Daughter Percentages of Isotope U-235			
Rock Layer	Percentage of U-235	Absolute Age	Period
G	94		
F	90		
D	65		
B	60		

3. Study the graph Half-Life of U-235 below. The half-life graph is plotted on a logarithmic scale, which straightens the curved line for radioactive decay. This scale can make it easier to plot data, as well as easier to use when the parent-daughter ratio represents less than a single half-life. Use the graph to determine the absolute ages of the rock layers in the chart.

Half-Life of U-235

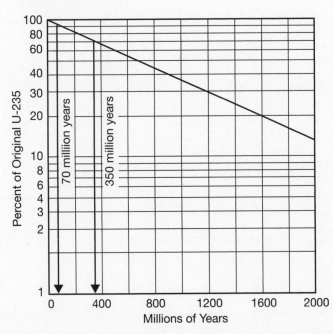

4. It takes 713 million years for half of a sample of U-235 to decay to lead-207. Use the Geologic Time Scale (Resource 10 in the DataBank) to complete Date Table 1 with the period during which each rock layer formed.

Part C: Understanding Index Fossils

5. Complete Data Table 2 below using the Geologic Time Scale
   (Resource 10) and the Key to Index Fossils (Resource 11) in the
   DataBank to determine approximate absolute ages for the rock
   layers in the block diagram (Figure 1) that display index fossils.

DATA TABLE 2

Approximate Age of Index Fossils			
Rock Layer	Index Fossil	Period	Approximate Age
C			
E			
A			

Analysis and Conclusions

1. **Applying Concepts** Which law, principle, or doctrine of relative
   dating did you apply to determine the relative ages of rock layers H
   and I?

   _____

2. **Applying Concepts** Which law, principle, or doctrine of relative
   dating did you apply to determine the relative ages of fault M and
   rock layer F?

   _____

3. **Applying Concepts** Explain how you know that fault N is older
   than the igneous intrusion J.

   _____

4. **Inferring** Why are there no index fossils in the granite and the
   basalt?

   _____

5. **Applying Concepts** How did you determine the sequence of the
   three igneous intrusions?

   _____

   _____

   _____

6. **Problem Solving** How is it possible for two distinct rock layers to
   derive from the same period?

   _____

   _____

Modeling the Ocean Floor

Introduction

The elevation of mountains is always expressed in terms of sea level. For example, Mount Everest rises 8848 m above sea level. But did you know the ocean floor is not actually level? Ocean basins have a variety of features including chains of volcanoes, tall mountain ranges, trenches, and large submarine plateaus.

Measuring the ocean floor from space has led scientists to a better understanding of the ocean floor. Data from orbiting satellites like the *TOPEX/Poseidon* and *Jason-1* reveal small-scale differences in ocean-surface height caused by ocean-floor features. Gravity attracts water toward regions where massive ocean-floor features occur—mountain ranges produce elevated areas of the ocean surface, and trenches cause slight depressions. Satellites are able to measure these small differences by bouncing microwaves off the ocean surface.

Scientists can use the sea-surface measurements produced by satellites and traditional sonar depth measurements to create detailed maps of ocean-floor features. These maps aren't generally accurate enough to produce navigational charts. But they are useful for many other purposes such as determining how undersea structures affect ocean currents and finding shallow seamounts where fish might be abundant.

In this investigation, you will create a three-dimensional model of the ocean floor, using a map derived from satellite data.

Problem

How can you model the ocean floor, using maps created from satellite data?

Pre-Lab Discussion

Read the entire investigation. Then work with a partner to answer the following questions.

1. **Posing Questions** Write a question that summarizes the purpose of this investigation.

   _____

   _____

   _____

2. **Predicting** How will you represent each depth on your model?

   _____

   _____

   _____

3. **Designing Experiments** What is the purpose of the small pieces of corrugated cardboard you will place between the contour layers on your model?

_____

_____

_____

4. **Inferring** What is one advantage of the model? What is one disadvantage of the map?

_____

_____

_____

5. **Inferring** Based on the data on the map, do you believe you will be able to create an accurate model of the ocean floor? Explain your answer.

_____

_____

_____

Materials *(per pair of students)*

Resource 4 in the DataBank

Resource 5 in the DataBank

tracing paper

thin cardboard

thick, corrugated cardboard

large piece of cardboard (9 in. × 11 in.)

scissors

glue

tempera paint

plastic gloves

Safety 🔪 🧥 🧤 🧫 🔥

Put on a laboratory apron. Use care with the scissors, especially when cutting through corrugated cardboard. Wear plastic gloves and take care when using the paints. Wash your hands after using the paints. Note all safety symbols next to the steps in the Procedure and review the meanings of each symbol by referring to the symbol guide on page xiii.

Procedure

1. Place the tracing paper over the image of the mid-ocean ridge in the Southern Ocean. Trace around each color. Each tracing represents one contour, which means the depth for that area is the same.

2. Use the scale to determine the depth (in km) represented by each color. Write the depth each of your tracings represents.

3. Trace each contour line from the tracing paper onto a piece of thin cardboard. Cut out each one.

4. Put on your lab apron and rubber gloves. Choose a color to represent each depth. Paint each area the color you have chosen to correspond to that depth.

5. On the side of the large piece of cardboard, make a key for the color you chose to represent each depth. You will build your model on this piece of cardboard. Wash your hands when you have finished painting.

6. Cut out small squares of corrugated cardboard to place between each layer of your model.

7. Create your model by stacking each contour in order of depth. Place corrugated cardboard between the contour layers to provide relief.

8. Carefully glue your model together.

Analysis and Conclusions

1. **Observing** Check the scale of your model. How do the numbers correspond with height of the ocean floor features? Explain your answer.

   _____

   _____

   _____

2. **Inferring** Imagine you made a similar model from a topographic map of an area of land. How would these numbers correspond with the height of the land features? Explain your answer.

   _____

   _____

   _____

3. **Observing** What is the contour interval for your model?

   _____

4. **Inferring** The map from which you created your model was derived from satellite measurements of sea-surface levels. These levels vary by only about 60 cm. How do you think scientists can determine these depth differences in kilometers?

_____

_____

_____

5. **Inferring** Large-scale ocean currents and eddies also affect the height of the sea surface. How do you think scientists can gain reliable information about the ocean floor topography from satellite data?

_____

_____

_____

6. **Applying Concepts** How could scientists check to be certain that the ocean-floor maps they are generating from satellite data are accurate?

_____

_____

_____

_____

_____

7. **Applying Concepts** How could you have improved the model you made in this exercise?

_____

_____

Go Further

Using the library or Internet, research the value of satellite-generated data for determining the motion of currents in the world oceans. How is the motion of currents related to ocean-floor topography?

Shoreline Features

Introduction

Shorelines come in many forms—from the steep Pacific cliffs to sandy
barrier beaches along the Atlantic. Geologists have developed two
general classifications for coasts that are based on how the land is
affected by past changes in sea level.

Emergent coasts result from rising land or falling sea level. They
are characterized by **wave-cut cliffs** or **platforms. Submergent coasts**
result from rising sea level or sinking land. These often feature
estuaries resulting from flooded river mouths. Both coast types
experience wave erosion and deposition of sediments. Therefore, you
can find similar features in all coastal areas. Some of these features
include **beaches, spits, tombolos,** and **baymouth bars.**

In this investigation, you will identify coastal features and analyze
how they formed. You will also determine how man-made features
designed to stabilize the shore affect natural erosion and deposition
processes.

Problem

How can you identify and analyze shoreline features?

Pre-Lab Discussion

*Read the entire investigation. Then work with a partner to answer the
following questions.*

1. **Posing Questions** Write a question that summarizes the purpose
   of this investigation.

   _____

   _____

   _____

2. **Inferring** How are the diagrams, maps, and aerial views helpful to
   this investigation?

   _____

   _____

   _____

3. **Inferring** Why do all shorelines share similarities?

   _____

   _____

   _____

Materials (per pair of students)
Figures 1, 2, and 3

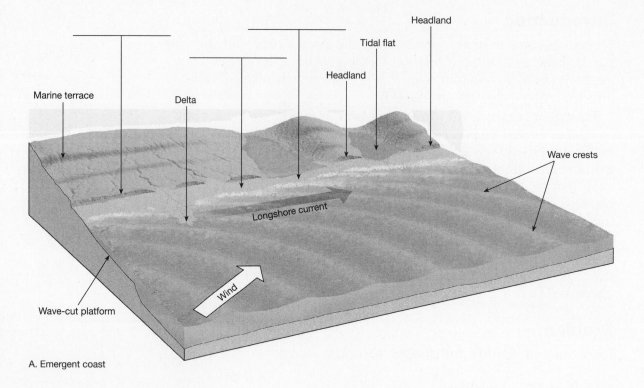

Marine terrace

Delta

Headland

Tidal flat

Headland

Wave crests

Longshore current

Wind

Wave-cut platform

A. Emergent coast

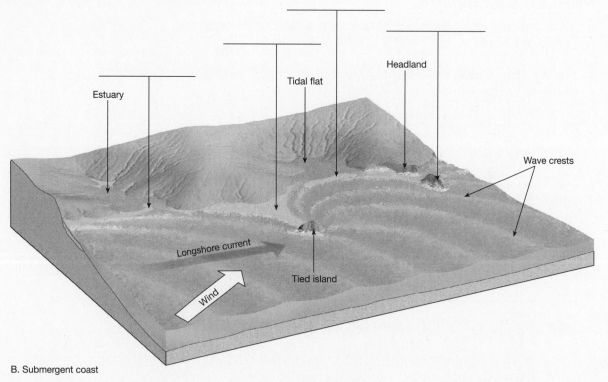

Estuary

Tidal flat

Headland

Wave crests

Longshore current

Tied island

Wind

B. Submergent coast

Figure 1

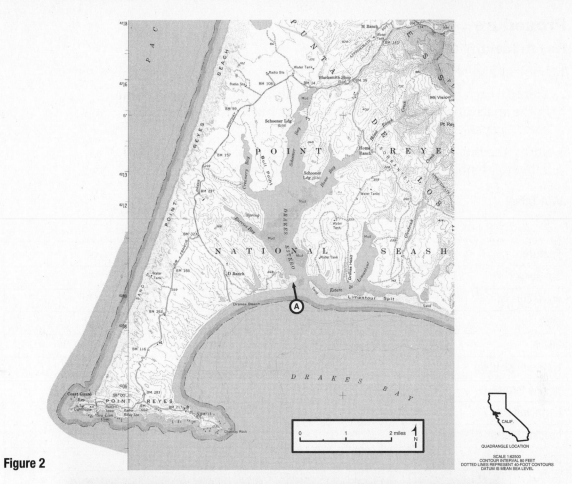

Figure 2

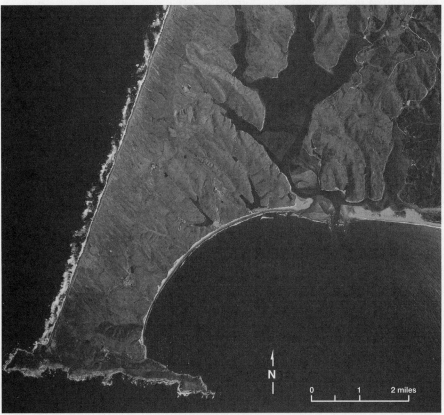

Figure 3

Procedure

Part A: Identify Coastal Features

1. Look at Figure 1.

2. Identify each of the following coastal features by writing the name in the space above the appropriate arrow: *barrier island, tombolo, beach, spit, sea stack, baymouth bar, wave-cut cliff.*

3. Study the illustrations in Figure 1. Use them to complete the Data Table to identify which process formed each feature.

DATA TABLE

Classifying Shoreline Features	
Feature	**Process**
sea stack	
wave-cut cliff	
delta	
beach	
wave-cut platform	
marine terrace	
baymouth bar	
headland	
spit	
tombolo	
barrier island	

Part B: Identify Current Directions

4. Contrast the topographic map of a portion of Point Reyes, California, in Figure 2 with the high-altitude image of the same area in Figure 3.

5. Indicate the direction of the current in the vicinity of Limantour Spit by drawing a large arrow.

Analysis and Conclusions

1. **Observing** Explain how you determined the current direction near Limantour Spit. Use Figures 2 and 3 to explain your answer.

_____

_____

_____

_____

2. **Observing** Is the Point Reyes area a submergent or emergent coast? Explain your reasoning using specific features on the map and image.

_____

_____

_____

_____

_____

3. **Applying Concepts** Imagine you were an engineer seeking to restore boat access to the lagoon in the emergent coast in Figure 1. What structure would you build and where would you build it? Explain your answer.

_____

_____

_____

4. **Applying Concepts** Point Reyes, a typical headland, is undergoing severe wave erosion. What type of features are Chimney Rock and the other rocks located off the shore of Point Reyes? How did the features form?

_____

_____

_____

_____

5. Predicting What will eventually happen to the land at the tip of Point Reyes?

_____

_____

_____

_____

6. Inferring Imagine somebody constructed a groin by the word "Limantour" on Limantour Spit. On which side of the groin, east or west, will sand accumulate? What will be the effect on the opposite side of the groin?

_____

_____

_____

_____

7. Inferring How did the U-shaped lake east of D Ranch form?

_____

_____

_____

8. Applying Concepts What is the feature labeled *A* on the map?

_____

Go Further

Coastal features are either helpful or harmful to navigation. Use the library or the Internet to find either an instance of a boater who ran into trouble due to a coastal feature or a boater who was saved by the presence of a coastal feature. Report your findings in the form of a news article.

Chapter 17   The Atmosphere: Structure and Temperature   **Investigation 17A**

Determining How Temperature Changes with Altitude

Introduction

The atmosphere is divided into four layers based on temperature: the **troposphere,** the **stratosphere,** the **mesosphere,** and the **thermosphere.** The temperature in the lower 12 km of the atmosphere decreases with altitude. However, at altitudes from about 12 to 45 km, the temperature increases.

In this investigation, you will explore the temperature changes in Earth's atmosphere as altitude increases and investigate what causes these temperature changes.

Problem

How does the temperature of Earth's atmosphere change with altitude?

Pre-Lab Discussion

Read the entire investigation. Then work with a partner to answer the following questions.

1. **Posing Questions** Write a question that summarizes the purpose of this investigation.

   _____

   _____

   _____

2. **Inferring** What are the possible sources of heat for the atmosphere?

   _____

   _____

   _____

3. **Predicting** What substance in the upper atmosphere is important to temperature changes in the upper atmospheric layers?

   _____

   _____

   _____

Name _____ Class _____ Date _____

Materials *(per group of students)*
ruler or straight edge
colored pencils
tracing paper
Resource 12 in the DataBank

Procedure
1. Carefully study the Atmospheric Temperature Curve shown in Resource 12.

2. Using tracing paper and the ruler, trace Resource 12.

3. Use the ruler to draw in the lines for the tropopause, stratopause, and mesopause. Label each line. If necessary, use your textbook as a reference.

4. Label the troposphere, mesosphere, stratosphere, and thermosphere.

5. Shade in each section. Use a different color for each section.

Analysis and Conclusions
1. **Using Graphs** What is the approximate temperature of the atmosphere at each of the following altitudes?

 10 km: _____ °C

 50 km: _____ °C

 80 km: _____ °C

2. **Using Graphs** How does the temperature change with altitude in the troposphere?

 _____

 _____

 _____

3. **Drawing Conclusions** What causes the temperature change in the troposphere?

 _____

 _____

 _____

4. **Using Graphs** How does the temperature change with altitude in the stratosphere?

 _____

 _____

Name _____ Class _____ Date _____

5. Drawing Conclusions What causes the temperature change in the stratosphere?

_____

_____

_____

6. Using Graphs How does the temperature change with altitude in the mesosphere and thermosphere?

_____

_____

_____

_____

7. Drawing Conclusions Explain the temperature change with altitude in the thermosphere.

_____

_____

_____

_____

8. Calculating If the average normal temperature decrease with altitude in the troposphere is 6.5°C/km, calculate the approximate temperature at 6,000 m if the surface temperature is 16°C. Show your work.

9. Calculating If the average or normal temperature decrease with altitude in the troposphere is 6.5°C/km, calculate the approximate altitude in which a pilot would expect to find each of the following atmospheric temperatures, if the surface temperature is 27°C. Show your work.

10°C: _____ meters

0°C: _____ meters

10. Inferring Of what importance is the gas ozone in the
stratosphere? How would a decrease of ozone in the stratosphere
affect the radiation received at Earth's surface?

_____

_____

_____

Go Further

Temperature measurements from the upper atmosphere are gathered
by using weather balloons. The balloons collect data on temperature,
humidity, and wind. The temperature data are plotted versus
pressure/height on plots called Skew-T diagrams that provide
information on the vertical structure of the atmosphere. Compare
diagrams from different areas to help answer the following questions.
Is the vertical temperature profile of the atmosphere the same
everywhere at all times? What can cause the temperature profile to
change?

Investigating Factors That Control Temperature

Introduction

One summer day, the official temperature in Columbus, Ohio, was reported as 88°F. However, the electronic sign at a local drugstore reported a temperature of 97°F. Was the temperature on the sign wrong? Actually, both measurements were correct, but they were measured under different conditions.

Official temperatures are measured in the shade, over a grassy surface, and five feet above the ground. The store's temperature was measured by a sensor in full sun, located close to a dark, paved surface. This difference in measuring the temperature accounted for almost a 10-degree increase in temperature—on the same day and at the same time.

In this investigation, you will explore the differences in temperature across North America and investigate the factors that influence temperature.

Problem

How does temperature vary and what causes these variations?

Pre-Lab Discussion

Read the entire investigation. Then work with a partner to answer the following questions.

1. **Posing Questions** Write a question that summarizes the purpose of this investigation.

   _____

   _____

   _____

2. **Inferring** What factors can influence temperature?

   _____

   _____

   _____

3. **Predicting** Which heats up faster, land or water?

   _____

   _____

   _____

Materials *(per group of students)*

ruler or straight edge

graph paper

Resources 14 and 15 in the DataBank

Procedure

1. Study Resource 14. The top map shows surface temperature across the United States, and it has been contoured to show areas that have the same temperature range. The contour lines are similar to the contour lines shown on a topographic map. However, these contour lines represent temperature rather than elevation.

2. Locate your state on Resource 14. Use the scale below the map to determine the temperature range or ranges that occurred in your state on August 9, 2004.

   _____

   _____

3. Make a temperature profile, or cross section, from the southwest corner of New Mexico through the Four Corners to the northeast corner of Colorado. The Four Corners is the location where the borders of New Mexico, Arizona, Utah, and Colorado intersect. First place a piece of paper on the United States map on Resource 14, extending from the SW corner of New Mexico to the NE corner of Colorado. Mark the ends of the cross section.

4. Then make marks on the paper where contour lines cross the profile line. Label the areas in between the marks with the corresponding temperature ranges from the map scale.

5. Use the marks to construct a temperature profile across this area on graph paper. Make the horizontal scale of the graph double the horizontal scale of the map.

6. Use the contour plots on Resources 14 and 15 in the DataBank (United States Surface Temperature, North American Surface Temperature, 24-Hour Temperature Change, and Surface Heat Index) to answer the questions in **Analysis and Conclusions.**

Analysis and Conclusions

1. **Using Graphs** How does the temperature profile you made across New Mexico and Colorado change?

   _____

   _____

   _____

   _____

Name _____ Class _____ Date _____

[blank boxed area]

2. Observing What are the lowest temperatures shown on the North American Surface Temperature Contour Plot on Resource 14? What are the highest temperatures?

_____
_____
_____

3. Inferring Which coast of North America is the leeward coast and which is the windward coast?

_____
_____

4. Inferring Which coast, leeward or windward, usually has cooler temperatures? Explain. Does the data shown on both maps on Resource 14 support this inference?

_____
_____
_____

5. Analyzing Data What is the general trend of temperature shown on the North American Surface Temperature Contour Plot?

_____
_____
_____

Name _____ Class _____ Date _____

6. Analyzing Data On the maps on Resources 14, there is a band of cooler temperatures that extends from northern New Mexico through Colorado, and up into Wyoming, Montana, and Idaho. What do you think could be influencing this area of cooler temperatures?

_____

_____

_____

_____

7. Analyzing Data Use the 24-hour temperature change contour plot on Resource 15 to determine where in the United States the temperature change over the 24-hour period was the greatest. Was the temperature change positive or negative?

_____

_____

_____

_____

8. Analyzing Concepts Study the heat index contour plot on Resource 15. The heat index is used to warn people when temperatures are high enough to pose a health hazard. The heat index combines the air temperature with relative humidity to determine the apparent temperature—what the air temperature "feels like" to the average person. A heat index of 90°F–105°F with prolonged exposure or physical activity can cause sunstroke or heat exhaustion, which can be dangerous to health. Where in the United States should people be warned about the possible danger of prolonged outdoor physical activity?

_____

_____

_____

Go Further

Investigate the current temperatures, heat index, or wind chill in your area by accessing temperature plots available on the Internet. Your teacher will provide you with the Web site information or with copies of the current data. Which features in your area have a strong influence on local temperature?

Earth Science Lab Manual ▪ **114**

Chapter 18   Moisture, Clouds, and Precipitation   Investigation 18

Recipe for a Cloud

Introduction

Clouds are a form of condensation, and they are best described as visible mixtures of tiny deposits of water or tiny crystals of ice. **Condensation** is the process of water vapor changing to a liquid state. For example, on a hot, muggy day, water droplets form on a cool glass of lemonade—that's condensation. **Evaporation** is the process of a liquid changing to a gas at the liquid's surface. A puddle you see in the morning that is gone by the afternoon is an example of evaporation.

When you use a hand pump to inflate a bicycle tire, the metal pump cylinder feels warm when you have finished. Its temperature increases when air is compressed. If you hold your hand just above the tire valve while you release the air, the escaping air feels cool. That cooling is caused by expanding air. This cooling and warming of air is caused by pressure changes called **adiabatic temperature changes.**

A raging forest fire sends plumes of smoke high into the sky. The smoke particles become surfaces to which liquid water can stick. The surfaces are called **condensation nuclei.**

In this investigation, you will examine the formation of clouds and the roles played by temperature changes, humidity, and the presence of tiny particles.

Problem

What are the necessary processes and conditions for cloud formation?

Pre-Lab Discussion

Read the entire investigation. Then work with a partner to answer the following questions.

1. **Forming Hypotheses** Write a hypothesis that explains how pressure, humidity, and the presence of tiny particles in the air contribute to cloud formation.

   _____

   _____

   _____

2. **Designing Experiments** Why is it important to use a container in which the pressure can be easily and significantly changed?

   _____

   _____

   _____

3. Controlling Variables When the cold water is used, what is the independent variable?

_____

_____

_____

4. Controlling Variables When the hot water is used, how does it affect cloud formation?

_____

_____

_____

Materials (per group)

graduated cylinder

gallon glass pickle jar

plastic freezer storage bag (26 cm × 26 cm)

rubber band (15-cm circumference; 0.5-cm width)

cold tap water

hot tap water

safety matches

Safety 🔥 ⚡ ⚠ ⚠ 🔥

Put on safety goggles. Be careful to avoid breakage when handling glassware. Be careful when using matches. Do not reach over an open flame. Tie back loose hair and clothing when working with flames. Note all safety symbols next to the steps in the Procedure and review the meaning of each symbol by referring to the symbols guide on page xiii.

Procedure

⚠ 1. Use the graduated cylinder to measure 40 mL of cold water. Pour the water into the jar. Place the plastic bag into the jar so that the top edges of the bag lie just outside the rim of the jar, as shown in Figure 1. **CAUTION:** *Wipe up any spilled liquids immediately to avoid slips and falls.*

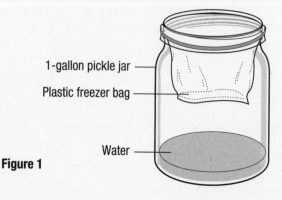

1-gallon pickle jar

Plastic freezer bag

Water

Figure 1

2. Secure the top of the bag to the outer rim of the jar using the rubber band, as shown in Figure 2.

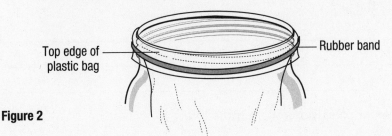

Top edge of plastic bag

Rubber band

Figure 2

3. Put your hand inside the bag and grab the bottom edge of the bag. Rapidly pull the bag out of the jar. Carefully watch the inside of the jar after pulling the bag out. Record your observations in the Data Table.

4. Remove the rubber band and plastic bag. Light a match and allow it to burn for about 3 seconds. Drop the match into the jar. Quickly place the plastic bag inside the jar and secure its top edge around the rim of the jar with the rubber band. **CAUTION:** *Be careful when using matches.*

5. Repeat Step 3. Carefully watch the inside of the jar after you rapidly pull the bag out of the jar. Record your observations in the Data Table.

6. Remove the plastic bag and rinse out the bottle. Throw away the burned match as directed by your teacher.

7. Repeat Steps 1 through 6 using 40 mL of hot tap water. **CAUTION:** *Be careful not to burn yourself when using hot water and matches.*

Observations

DATA TABLE

Water Type	Smoke	Cloud Formation
Cold	Absent	
Cold	Present	
Hot	Absent	
Hot	Present	

If clouds formed under more than one set of conditions, did you observe any difference between the clouds?

_____

_____

_____

Analysis and Conclusions

1. **Inferring** What effect did pulling the plastic bag out of the jar have on the water vapor inside the jar?

   _____

   _____

   _____

2. **Drawing Conclusions** What conditions were most likely to produce clouds?

   _____

   _____

   _____

3. **Drawing Conclusions** Did your results support your hypothesis? Explain your answer.

   _____

   _____

   _____

4. **Using Models** In this investigation, you observed several factors that contributed to cloud formation. How does each of these factors occur in nature?

   _____

   _____

   _____

   _____

5. **Designing Experiments** How could you improve upon the design of this investigation to better model the process of cloud formation in nature?

   _____

   _____

   _____

Analyzing Pressure Systems

Introduction

Wind is caused by differences in pressure. Wind forms as air moves from areas of high pressure to areas of low pressure.

In a **low-pressure system** in the Northern Hemisphere, winds blow inward in a counterclockwise direction. Air pressure is lowest in the center of the system.

In a **high-pressure system** in the Northern Hemisphere, winds blow outward in a clockwise direction. Pressure is highest in the center of the system.

In this investigation, you will identify wind patterns and predict the movement of pressure systems.

Problem

How do wind patterns relate to pressure systems?

Pre-Lab Discussion

Read the entire investigation. Then work with a partner to answer the following questions.

1. **Posing Questions** Write a question that summarizes the purpose of this investigation.

   _____

   _____

   _____

2. **Designing Experiments** In which direction will your arrows point around low-pressure systems? In which direction will they point around high-pressure systems?

   _____

   _____

3. **Inferring** Why are low-pressure systems associated with areas of air movement?

   _____

   _____

   _____

Name _____ Class _____ Date _____

Materials *(per student pair)*
colored pencils

Procedure

1. Sketch the outline of your school building in the blank box below.

2. On a windy day, go outside with your partner and stand with the wind to your back. Slowly walk around the school until you reach an area where you feel the air movement increase or a slight counterclockwise swirl. This location is a small area of low pressure.

3. On your drawing of your school, use a red pencil to write an *L* to mark the area of low pressure.

4. To find small areas of high pressure, slowly walk around the school with the wind in your face until you feel the air grow suddenly still.

5. On your drawing of your school, use a blue pencil to write an *H* to mark the area of high pressure.

6. Walk around the entire perimeter of your school, marking areas of highs and lows on your drawing. Stay within 10 meters of the school.

7. On your sketch of the school, draw arrows indicating the movement of air around the low-pressure systems and high-pressure systems.

8. Figure 1 shows wind direction for a large low-pressure system. When the wind is blowing from the north, the center of the low-pressure system lies to the east of you.

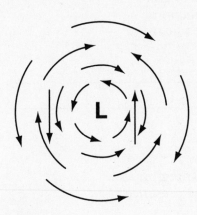

Figure 1

Analysis and Conclusions

1. **Analyzing Data** Describe the general location of low- and high-pressure systems around your school building.

_____

_____

_____

2. **Comparing and Contrasting** Compare your sketches to those of other students. Were the low- and high-pressure systems located in the same places around the school? Why or why not?

_____

_____

_____

3. **Interpreting Diagrams** Using Figure 1, if the wind is blowing from the south, where is the low-pressure system relative to your location?

_____

_____

4. **Interpreting Diagrams** Using Figure 1, if the wind is blowing from the southwest, where is the low-pressure system relative to your location?

_____

_____

5. **Inferring** In general, weather systems move from west to east across the United States. Knowing this, which wind direction would indicate that a low-pressure system was headed toward your area?

_____

_____

Go Further

Obtain a U.S. weather map and a weather forecast for your region from a newspaper or the Internet. Relate the forecast to the presence of high- or low-pressure systems.

Analyzing Severe Weather Data

Introduction

Tornadoes are violent windstorms associated with severe thunderstorms. Meteorologists carefully monitor atmospheric data to predict where thunderstorms might develop. They also attempt to predict whether these storms might spawn powerful tornadoes. To aid them in this task, meteorologists use thermodynamic indices.

Thermodynamic indices are sets of numbers that indicate the state of the atmosphere at a given time and place. Three important thermodynamic indices are the dew-point index, the lifted index, and the storm relative helicity index.

The **dew-point index** indicates the amount of moisture in the atmosphere. The dew-point temperature of an area usually needs to be at least 50°F for a tornado to develop.

The **lifted index** indicates how fast or slow air is rising or sinking. Air must be rising for a thunderstorm—and therefore, a tornado—to develop.

The **storm relative helicity index** indicates whether or not the air is rotating. For a tornado to develop, air must be turned or spun as it rises.

In this investigation, you will use thermodynamic indices and weather maps to predict where a tornado might strike.

Problem

Where are tornadoes most likely to occur?

Pre-Lab Discussion

Read the entire investigation. Then work with a partner to answer the following questions.

1. **Posing Questions** Write a question that summarizes the purpose of this lab.

   _____

   _____

   _____

2. **Forming Definitions** What is the dew-point index? For the purposes of this investigation, how does it relate to tornadoes?

   _____

   _____

   _____

3. Formulating Hypotheses What conditions are most favorable for the development of a tornado?

_____

_____

Materials *(per pair of students)*
3 colored pencils

Procedure
Part A: Analyzing Dew-Point Index
1. Study the weather map in Figure 1. The map shows dew-point temperatures in the United States on April 6, 2003.

2. Choose a colored pencil and shade in the states that have dew-point temperatures that are conducive to the formation of tornadoes.

3. Make a list of the shaded states. If you need help with the names of the states, use Figure 4, the labeled map of the United States.

_____

_____

Part B: Analyzing Lifted Index
4. Study the weather map in Figure 2. The map shows the lifted index for the United States on April 6, 2003. Data Table 1 includes a scale for the lifted index.

5. Choose a different colored pencil and shade in the states whose lifted indices are conducive to the formation of tornadoes.

6. Make a list of the shaded states. If you need help with the names of the states, use Figure 4, the labeled map of the United States.

_____

_____

Part C: Analyzing Storm Relative Helicity Index
7. Study the weather map in Figure 3. The map shows the storm relative helicity index for the United States on April 6, 2003. Data Table 2 includes a scale for this index.

8. Choose a different colored pencil and shade in the states whose storm relative helicity values are conducive to the formation of tornadoes.

9. Make a list of the shaded states. If you need help with the names of the states, use Figure 4, the labeled map of the United States.

_____

_____

Name _____ Class _____ Date _____

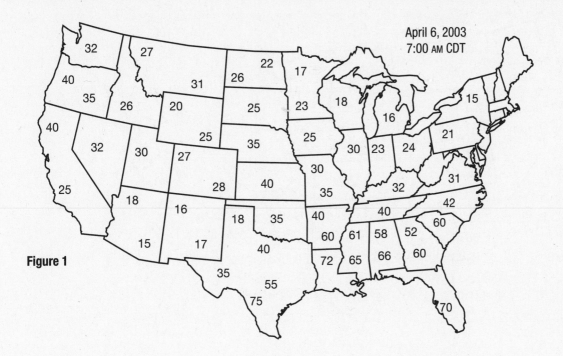

Figure 1

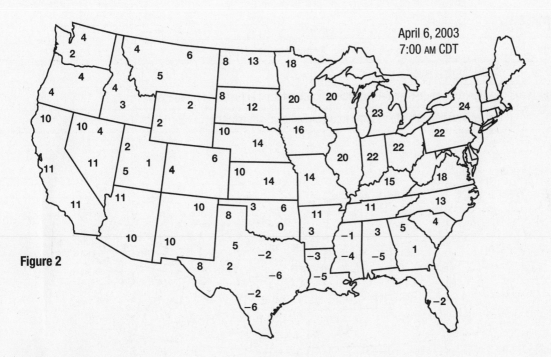

Figure 2

DATA TABLE 1

Lifted Index	Stability
> 0	Air is sinking; very stable atmosphere
0	Stable atmosphere
−1 to −3	Slightly unstable (severe thunderstorms most likely)
−4 to −5	Unstable (severe storms, hail, maybe smaller tornadoes)
< −6	Very unstable (severe storms, larger hail, possibly larger tornadoes)

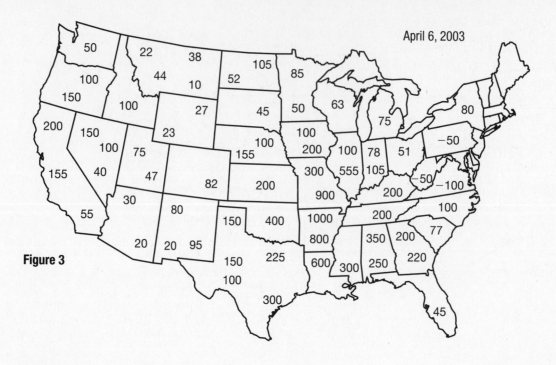

Figure 3

April 6, 2003

DATA TABLE 2

Helicity	Amount of Rotation
> 100	Some storm rotation
> 250	Enough rotation to support supercell thunderstorms and some tornadoes
> 400	Enough rotation to support dangerous tornadic thunderstorms

Figure 4

Name _____ Class _____ Date _____

Analysis and Conclusions

1. **Interpreting Diagrams** Considering only the dew-point data, in which states could a tornado have possibly formed on April 3, 2003?

_____

_____

_____

2. **Analyzing Data** Considering only the lifted index data, in which states could a tornado have possibly formed on April 3, 2003?

_____

_____

3. **Interpreting Diagrams** Based only on the storm relative helicity data, in which states could a tornado have possibly formed on April 3, 2003?

_____

_____

_____

4. **Predicting** Study your combined data, then predict which states are most likely to have experienced a tornado.

_____

_____

5. **Evaluating and Revising** What criteria did you use to make your decision?

_____

_____

_____

6. **Applying Concepts** Imagine that a cold front moved across the southeastern United States on April 6, 2003. Would this front have increased or decreased the chances of tornado formation? Explain your answer.

_____

_____

_____

_____

Go Further

Thermodynamic indices are available on the Internet. Search the Internet for Web sites that post data about these indices. Select a state, then gather data about its dew point, lifted index, and storm relative helicity on one particular date. Predict whether the state is likely to experience a tornado.

Interpreting Weather Diagrams

Introduction

Every day meteorologists send weather balloons high into the atmosphere. These balloons carry weather instruments that record atmospheric conditions such as temperature, pressure, and wind speed. This information is transmitted to a computer, which then creates a printout called a Skew-T.

A **Skew-T** is a diagram that shows the condition of the atmosphere for a particular area at a particular time. It includes minor thermodynamic indices that provide valuable information to meteorologists.

In this investigation, you will use a Skew-T diagram to predict the possibility of severe weather.

Problem

How can thermodynamic indices be used to predict the possibility of a severe storm?

Pre-Lab Discussion

Read the entire investigation. Then work with a partner to answer the following questions.

1. **Controlling Variables** Why must all the data for Lake Charles be gathered at the same time and date?

   _____

   _____

   _____

2. **Forming Definitions** What information does the Bulk Richardson Number (BRN) provide?

   _____

   _____

3. **Predicting** What type of weather would you expect for an area with an energy index (EI) of 3?

   _____

   _____

4. **Formulating Hypotheses** Using the minor thermodynamic indices as a guide, what conditions are associated with severe weather?

   _____

   _____

   _____

Procedure

1. Study the Skew-T diagram in Figure 1. The Skew-T shows minor thermodynamic indices for Lake Charles, Louisiana, on April 6, 2003.

2. Locate the six indices listed in Data Table 1 on the Skew-T diagram. Write these indices in the Data Table.

3. Use the Skew-T diagram to fill in Data Table 2 with the corresponding value for each of the six indices.

4. Based on the values on the Skew-T and Data Table 1, complete Data Table 2 with the expected weather or conditions for Lake Charles on April 6, 2003.

April 6, 2003

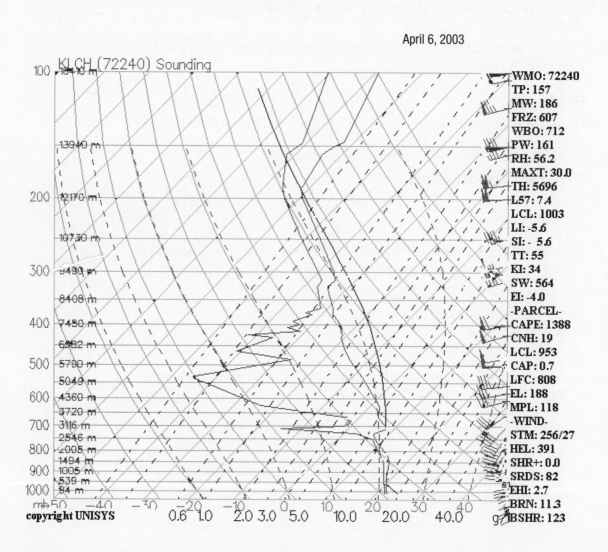

Figure 1

Name _____ Class _____ Date _____

DATA TABLE 1

TT	Type of Weather Expected
44–50	Thunderstorms are possible
51–52	Severe thunderstorms possible with isolated tornadoes
53–56	Numerous thunderstorms possible, some severe, a few tornadoes
> 56	Numerous severe thunderstorms, scattered tornadoes possible
SW	**Type of Storm**
> 300	Severe thunderstorms likely to occur
> 400	Tornadic thunderstorms likely to occur
EI	**Type of Weather Expected**
> 0	No storms expected
0 to −2	Isolated severe thunderstorms
< −2	Severe storms possible, isolated tornadoes
CAPE	**Amount of Energy/Buoyancy in the Atmosphere**
0–1500	Small amount
1500–2500	Moderate amount
2500–3500	Large amount
EHI	**Type of Storm**
< 1.0	Tornadic thunderstorms cannot be supported
> 1.0	Tornadic thunderstorms can be supported
BRN	**Type of Storm That Could Develop**
< 30	Storms may not form at all
30 to 60	Tornadic thunderstorms could develop
> 70	Thunderstorms with heavy rain

DATA TABLE 2

Indices	Corresponding Values	Expected Weather/Conditions

Analysis and Conclusions

1. **Interpreting Diagrams** What type of weather is associated with the Total totals (TT) for Lake Charles?

   _____

   _____

2. **Analyzing Data** Which of the indices for Lake Charles indicate severe weather? Which indices do not?

   _____

   _____

   _____

3. **Predicting** One can use the indices to make a rough approximation of whether atmospheric conditions could support the development of severe weather. Dividing the number of indices that indicate severe weather by the total number of indices and multiplying that number by 100 results in a percentage. Based on your data, what is the rough probability for atmospheric conditions that could support severe weather in Lake Charles? Show your work.

4. **Evaluating and Revising** Why is the method described in item 3 considered a rough approximation? Explain your answer.

   _____

   _____

   _____

   _____

Go Further

As with the three major thermodynamic indices, minor indices are available on the Internet. Search the Internet for Web sites that post data about minor indices. Select a city and then gather data about the following indices: TT, SW, EI, CAPE, EHI, and BRN. Predict whether the city is likely to experience severe weather.

Creating a Weather Station

Introduction

Meteorologists use numerous thermodynamic indices to help develop forecasts. Much of this information can be found on the Internet. In addition, the Internet is a good source for radar images that indicate wind speeds and storm locations. Satellite images that show differences in cloud temperatures and surface temperatures are also available on the Internet.

In this investigation, you will use data gathered from the Internet to create a weather station to make severe weather predictions. To complete this activity, you must review the thermodynamic indices discussed in the two previous labs.

Problem

How can data be organized into a weather station to make severe weather predictions?

Pre-Lab Discussion

Read the entire investigation. Review the information on thermodynamic indices in the two previous labs. Then work with a partner to answer the following questions.

1. **Forming Definitions** What does a storm relative helicity value of 250 mean?

   _____

   _____

2. **Predicting** What type of weather would you expect for an area that has a lifted index of −6?

   _____

   _____

3. **Predicting** What type of weather would you expect for an area with a severe weather threat (SW) of 460?

   _____

   _____

4. **Designing Experiments** How will you organize your weather station?

   _____

   _____

   _____

   _____

Name _____ Class _____ Date _____

Materials *(per pair of students)*
computer with Internet access
printer
labeled map of the United States
colored pencils

Procedure

Part A: Creating a Weather Station

1. In Internet Explorer, go to the menu bar and click on "Favorites." If you are using Netscape, go to the menu bar and click on "Bookmarks."

2. In Internet Explorer, click on "Organize Favorites." In Netscape, click on "Manage Bookmarks."

3. In Internet Explorer, click on "Create Folder," and name the new folder "Severe Weather Station." In Netscape, click on "File" in the menu bar, then "New," and lastly "Folder."

4. Move all the Web sites you bookmarked in the two previous labs into the Severe Weather Station folder.

5. Rename the Web sites. For example, a Web site that shows a dew-point map can be called "Dew-Point Index."

6. Your station should have the following named locations: Dew-Point Index, Lifted Index, Storm Relative Helicity Index, and Skew-T Diagrams. If necessary, conduct additional research. You can add additional Web sites that show frontal boundaries and radar and satellite images.

Part B: Gathering Weather Data

7. Using a site from your weather station, print out a U.S. weather map that shows dew-point temperatures. On the map in Figure 1, draw an outline around those states that have dew-point temperatures conducive to tornado formation.

8. Repeat Step 7 using different colored pencils for the lifted index and storm relative helicity index.

9. Determine which states meet the criteria for tornado formation for all three major indices.

10. Identify several cities within these states. Print out Skew-T diagrams for these cities using the sites from your weather station. Complete the Data Table with the corresponding values for the indices for each city.

Figure 1

DATA TABLE

City	Dewpoint	L. Index	Helicity	TT	SW	EI	CAPE	EHI	BRN

Analysis and Conclusions

1. **Interpreting Diagrams** Which states have dew-point temperatures that are conducive to tornado formation?

   _____

   _____

2. **Interpreting Diagrams** Which states have lifted indices that are conducive to tornado formation?

   _____

   _____

3. **Interpreting Diagrams** Which states have storm relative helicity values that are conducive to tornado formation?

   _____

   _____

4. **Analyzing Data** Based on your Skew-T diagrams, which of your chosen cities have at least three minor thermodynamic indices that indicate severe weather? Which cities do not have minor indices that indicate severe weather?

   _____

   _____

   _____

5. **Predicting** Based on your combined data, where is a tornado most likely to form?

   _____

   _____

   _____

6. **Evaluating and Revising** How do you think your prediction would change if you rechecked the data in several hours?

   _____

   _____

   _____

Go Further

Use the Internet to research caps, or temperature inversions. Explain what caps are. How do caps affect storm formation?

Modeling the Greenhouse Effect

Introduction

A greenhouse is a structure whose glass or plastic panes allow light from the sun to enter the structure but also prevent heat from escaping. In a similar way, Earth's atmosphere allows solar radiation to pass through it. Some of this radiation is absorbed by Earth's surface. Gases in the atmosphere, including carbon dioxide and water vapor, also absorb some of this energy and reflect it back to Earth's surface as heat. This greenhouse effect makes our planet's surface and atmosphere warmer than they would be otherwise.

In this investigation, you will model the greenhouse effect and compare your results to the greenhouse effect caused by Earth's atmosphere.

Problem

How can you model the greenhouse effect caused by Earth's atmosphere?

Pre-Lab Discussion

Read the entire investigation. Then work with a partner to answer the following questions.

1. **Posing Questions** Write a question that summarizes the purpose of this investigation.

   _____

   _____

2. **Controlling Variables** What is the dependent variable in this investigation?

   _____

   _____

3. **Controlling Variables** What is the independent variable in this investigation?

   _____

   _____

4. **Predicting** Based on the information given in the procedure, predict the outcome of this investigation.

   _____

   _____

Name _____ Class _____ Date _____

Materials (per pair of students)

2 clean, dry, transparent, 2-L
 plastic soda bottles with caps

laboratory burner

heat-resistant gloves

safety matches

large, metal knitting needle

2 identical, non-mercury,
 Celsius thermometers

modeling clay

direct sunlight or a
 gooseneck lamp
 with 100-W bulb

clock or watch

colored pencils

Safety 🔲🔲🔲🔲🔲🔲

Put on safety goggles. Tie back loose hair and clothing when working with flames. Do not reach over an open flame and keep alcohol away from any open flame. Also, be careful when using matches. Use extreme care when working with heated equipment or materials to avoid burns. Be careful to avoid breakage when working with the thermometers. Note all safety symbols next to the steps in the Procedure and review the meanings of each symbol by referring to the symbol guide on page xiii.

Procedure

1. Put on safety goggles.

2. Connect the laboratory burner to the gas valve.

3. Put on heat-resistant gloves and open the valve. Carefully light the burner and properly dispose of the match.

4. **CAUTION:** *Carefully warm the knitting needle in the flame and use it to make 30 holes in one of the 2-L bottles.* Distribute the holes evenly around the bottle, but do not make holes around the bottom 6 cm of the bottle. Turn off the burner and put it away.

5. Lower one thermometer into each of the bottles so that the bulbs of the thermometers are at the bottoms of the bottles. Screw the caps tightly onto the bottles.

6. Use the modeling clay to secure the bottles—upside down—in an area that gets direct sunlight or under the lamp. The bottles should be about 15 cm apart. If you are using a lamp, adjust the lamp so that each bottle is the same distance—about 10 cm— from the bulb.

7. Adjust the bottles so that the thermometers are set up the same way with respect to the light source.

8. If you are using a lamp as your light source, turn it on. **CAUTION:** *Lamps can get very hot. Do not move too close to the lamps when they are in use.* Measure the initial temperature shown on each thermometer and record these values in the data table.

9. Measure and record the temperature in each bottle every 5 minutes for 30 minutes.

Name _____ Class _____ Date _____

Observations

DATA TABLE

Time (minutes)	Temperature (°C)	
	Bottle Without Holes	**Perforated Bottle**
0		
5		
10		
15		
20		
25		
30		

GRAPH

Construct a line graph of your data on the grid below. Plot time, in minutes, on the horizontal axis, and temperature, in degrees Celsius, on the vertical axis. Use a different colored pencil to connect each set of data points. Include a key that indicates which set of data is which. Give your graph an appropriate title.

Title: _____

Key

Analysis and Conclusions

1. **Observing** In which of the two bottles did the temperature of the air rise at a faster rate? Explain why this happened.

   _____

   _____

2. **Relating Cause and Effect** In which of the bottles did the air reach the higher temperature? Why?

   _____

   _____

3. **Inferring** Which processes of heat transfer—conduction, radiation, convection—are involved in this activity?

   _____

4. **Using Analogies** Which bottle simulates the greenhouse effect caused by Earth's atmosphere? Why?

   _____

5. **Evaluating and Revising** What are some of the limitations of this model of Earth's greenhouse effect?

   _____

   _____

6. **Applying Concepts** How is the greenhouse effect related to global warming?

   _____

   _____

   _____

7. **Inferring** How could you alter the lab procedure to obtain better results?

   _____

   _____

   _____

Go Further

Compare your results from this investigation with the results from the Quick Lab in your textbook. Explain the effect of the greenhouse effect on air temperature alone, air temperature above soil, and air temperature above water.

Measuring the Angle of the Sun at Noon

Introduction

As Earth revolves around the sun, the orientation of Earth's axis to the sun continually changes. As a result, the location of the rising and setting sun changes throughout the year. The **altitude** is the angle above the horizon of the sun at noon. The altitude also changes throughout the year because of the orientation of Earth's axis.

In this investigation, you will indirectly observe the changing orientation of Earth's axis by measuring the altitude of the sun at noon over a period of several weeks.

Problem

How does the altitude of the sun at noon change over time?

Pre-Lab Discussion

Read the entire investigation. Then work with a partner to answer the following questions.

1. **Relating Cause and Effect** Does the sun actually move across the sky? Explain your answer.

_____

_____

_____

2. **Forming Definitions** What does the term *altitude* refer to in this investigation?

_____

_____

3. **Predicting** During what time of year would you expect the shadow of the meter stick to be longest? When would it be shortest?

_____

_____

_____

Name _____ Class _____ Date _____

Materials *(per student pair)*
2 meter sticks
calculator
protractor

Safety 🖾
Never look directly at the sun, as it may result in eye damage. Note the safety symbols next to the steps in the Procedure and review the meaning of each symbol by referring to the symbol guide on page xiii.

Procedure

1. On a sunny afternoon—noontime is best—go outside and find a flat, sunny area. Hold a meter stick upright with one end touching the ground, as shown in Figure 1. Use the protractor to make sure that the meter stick is perpendicular to the ground.

🖾 2. Observe the shadow cast by the meter stick. Hold the meter stick steady while your partner uses the other meter stick to measure the length of the shadow. **CAUTION:** *Never look directly at the sun, as it may result in eye damage.*

3. Using your calculator, divide the height of the meter stick by the length of the shadow. Record your calculations in Data Table 1.

4. Use Data Table 2 to determine the altitude of the sun at noon. Locate the number in the table that comes closest to your calculation in Step 3. Then record the corresponding angle in Data Table 1.

5. Complete Data Table 1 with the date and time of your observation of the sun's shadow.

6. Repeat Steps 1 through 5 at exactly the same time on several different days over a period of four or five weeks. Record your results in Data Table 1.

DATA TABLE 1

Observation	Date	Time	Calculations (Height of Meter Stick Divided by Length of Shadow)	Angle of Sun
1				
2				
3				
4				

Name _____ Class _____ Date _____

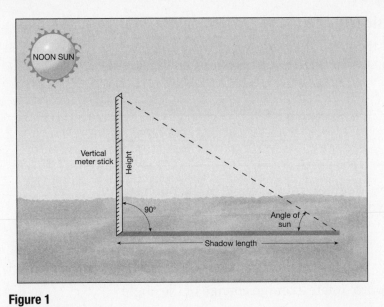

Figure 1

Data Table 2

If $\dfrac{\text{Height of Stick}}{\text{Length of Shadow}}$	Then Sun Angle is	If $\dfrac{\text{Height of Stick}}{\text{Length of Shadow}}$	Then Sun Angle is
0.2679	15°	1.235	51°
0.2867	16°	1.280	52°
0.3057	17°	1.327	53°
0.3249	18°	1.376	54°
0.3443	19°	1.428	55°
0.3640	20°	1.483	56°
0.3839	21°	1.540	57°
0.4040	22°	1.600	58°
0.4245	23°	1.664	59°
0.4452	24°	1.732	60°
0.4663	25°	1.804	61°
0.4877	26°	1.881	62°
0.5095	27°	1.963	63°
0.5317	28°	2.050	64°
0.5543	29°	2.145	65°
0.5774	30°	2.246	66°
0.6009	31°	2.356	67°
0.6249	32°	2.475	68°
0.6494	33°	2.605	69°
0.6745	34°	2.748	70°
0.7002	35°	2.904	71°
0.7265	36°	3.078	72°
0.7536	37°	3.271	73°
0.7813	38°	3.487	74°
0.8098	39°	3.732	75°
0.8391	40°	4.011	76°
0.8693	41°	4.332	77°
0.9004	42°	4.705	78°
0.9325	43°	5.145	79°
0.9657	44°	5.671	80°
1.0000	45°	6.314	81°
1.0360	46°	7.115	82°
1.0720	47°	8.144	83°
1.1110	48°	9.514	84°
1.1500	49°	11.430	85°
1.1920	50°		

Name _____ Class _____ Date _____

Analysis and Conclusions

1. **Analyzing Data** How did the altitude of the sun at noon—or the time you were able to measure the shadow of the sun—change over time?

   _____

   _____

   _____

2. **Analyzing Data** How many degrees did the angle of the noon sun change over the period of your observations?

   _____

   _____

3. **Calculating** What is the approximate average change of the angle of the noon sun per day?

   _____

   _____

4. **Relating Cause and Effect** Why does the angle of the noon sun change over time?

   _____

   _____

   _____

   _____

5. **Designing Experiments** How might you alter the procedure to get better results?

   _____

   _____

   _____

Go Further

Predict how your results would change if you repeated this investigation in six months.

Exploring Orbits

Introduction

In 1609, the German mathematician and astronomer Johannes Kepler deciphered a major puzzle of the solar system. The strange back-and-forth motions of the planets in the sky were nearly impossible to predict until Kepler figured out the true shapes of the planetary orbits around the sun. Orbits were always believed to be circular, but Kepler used mathematics to discover they were actually **elliptical.**

An **ellipse** is an oval that is characterized by two quantities. The first quantity is the width of the ellipse, which is called the **major axis.** The second quantity is called the **eccentricity,** which is a measure of how stretched out the ellipse is. Eccentricity is defined by the distance between two mathematically determined points within the ellipse called the foci.

For planets, one focus of their orbital ellipse is the sun. The other is an empty point in space. The orbit of each planet is an ellipse, but each planet's elliptical orbit has different major axes and eccentricities. Once Kepler understood the proper nature of orbits, the movements of the planets in the sky could be predicted with precision.

In this investigation, you will draw ellipses, calculate their eccentricities, observe an interesting property of ellipses, and compare the ellipses you draw with the orbital eccentricities of Earth and other planets in the solar system.

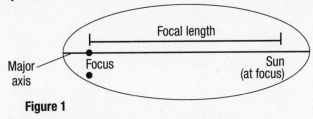

Figure 1

Problem

What do the elliptical orbits of the planets look like?

Pre-Lab Discussion

Read the entire investigation. Then work with a partner to answer the following questions.

1. **Predicting** Each planet's orbit is shaped like an ellipse. Predict whether the shapes of the planet's orbits will be more circular or more elongated.

_____

_____

_____

_____

2. Applying Concepts What is the one thing that the elliptical orbits
of all planets, asteroids, and most comets have in common?

_____

_____

_____

_____

3. Controlling Variables What is the independent variable for the
ellipses you will draw?

_____

_____

_____

_____

4. Controlling Variables What are the dependent variables for the
ellipses you will draw?

_____

_____

_____

_____

5. Designing Experiments What purpose do the two pushpins serve
in this investigation?

_____

_____

_____

_____

Materials *(per pair of students)*

3 sheets of paper
heavy corrugated cardboard (~50 cm × 60 cm)
2 pushpins
metric ruler
string, 30 cm long
5 colored pencils
cellophane tape
calculator

Name _____ Class _____ Date _____

Safety ✂

Be careful when handling sharp objects. Note all safety symbols next to the steps in the Procedure and review the meaning of each symbol by referring to the safety symbol guide on page xiii.

Procedure

Part A: Drawing Ellipses and Calculating Eccentricity

1. Fold a sheet of paper in half lengthwise. Flatten it out again.

✂ 2. Place the paper on the cardboard and measure 5 cm from the center of the page. Place one pushpin at the 5 cm mark. Measure 5 cm to the other side of the center of the paper and place a pushpin there. The pushpins should be 10 cm apart. **CAUTION:** *Be careful when handling the pins; they can puncture skin.*

3. Label one of the pushpins as the sun.

4. Tie the string in a loop and place it around the pins. Using one of the colored pencils, gently pull the string tight. Keep the string tight without pulling the pins out of the cardboard. Carefully drag the pencil around the pins to draw an ellipse, as shown in Figure 2.

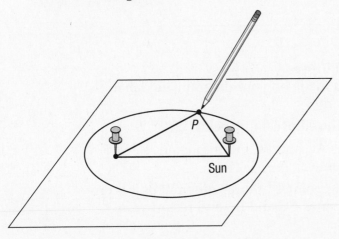

5. Using the same colored pencil, draw a circle around the pin that is not labeled as the sun. Remove the pin.

6. Use the metric ruler to measure the length of the major axis and focal length. Record these values in Data Table 1.

7. Reposition the second pin so that it is now 8.0 cm from the other pin. Repeat Steps 4 through 6, using a different colored pencil.

8. Repeat Step 7, using distances of 6.0 cm, 4.0 cm, and 2.0 cm between the pins. As the focal length for each ellipse becomes smaller, you may need to tape additional sheets of paper above and below the original sheet of paper to draw the entire ellipse.

9. The eccentricity for each ellipse is calculated by dividing the focal length by the length of the major axis:

$$\text{eccentricity} = \frac{\text{focal length}}{\text{major axis}}$$

Calculate the eccentricity for each ellipse. Record the values in Data Table 1.

10. Label each ellipse on your diagram with its matching eccentricity.

Observations

DATA TABLE 1

Ellipse (Color)	Major Axis (cm)	Focal Length (cm)	Eccentricity

Part B: Observing Properties of Ellipses

11. Choose one of the ellipses you made on your diagram and label the foci "A" and "B" respectively.

12. Choose a point anywhere on the ellipse and label it "C."

13. Measure the length of the lines AC and BC in centimeters. Record your measurements in Data Table 2.

14. Repeat Steps 12 and 13, placing point C at three different points on the ellipse. Carefully measure lines AC and BC and record your measurements in Data Table 2.

DATA TABLE 2

Position of C	Length of AC	Length of BC	Length of AC + BC
1			
2			
3			
4			

Analysis and Conclusions

1. **Compare and Contrast** Compare the following values for planetary eccentricities to those you calculated for your ellipses. What can you state about the orbits of the various planets?

   _____

   _____

   _____

   _____

Planet	Eccentricity
Mercury	0.206
Venus	0.007
Earth	0.017
Mars	0.093
Jupiter	0.048
Saturn	0.056
Uranus	0.047
Neptune	0.009
Pluto	0.250

2. **Inferring** What shape would you make if both pushpins were placed at a single central point? What would be the focal length and eccentricity of this shape?

   _____

   _____

   _____

3. **Observing** What did you discover in Part B about the sums of lines AC and BC for your ellipse? Generalize your findings as a "basic law of ellipses."

   _____

   _____

   _____

   _____

4. Drawing Conclusions Did your results from this activity confirm your original prediction? Explain why or why not.

_____

_____

_____

_____

5. Inferring What body in the solar system do you think is one focus of the moon's orbit?

_____

_____

_____

6. Inferring How would you modify this activity to offer a better sense of planetary orbits?

_____

_____

_____

_____

Go Further

Research the orbits of smaller bodies in the solar system such as asteroids or comets. Use the materials from this investigation and researched values for the major axis and eccentricity to produce drawings of the orbits of these objects. Include in your report your drawings and all values used.

Measuring the Diameter of the Sun

Introduction

The sun is approximately 150,000,000 km from Earth. To understand how far away this is, consider the fact that light travels approximately 300,000 km/s. At this speed, it takes the light from the sun a little more than eight minutes to reach Earth.

Even though the sun is extremely far away, it is still possible to make an approximate measurement of its size. The sun's diameter can be estimated by making two simple measurements and then solving a proportion problem.

$$\frac{\text{diameter of sun}}{\text{distance to sun}} = \frac{\text{diameter of sun's image}}{\text{distance between two cards}}$$

If you can determine three of the terms in the proportion problem, the fourth term, the diameter of the sun, can be solved mathematically.

In this investigation, you will construct a simple device and use it to collect data that will enable you to calculate the diameter of the sun.

Problem

What is the diameter of the sun and how can it be determined?

Pre-Lab Discussion

Read the entire investigation. Then work with a partner to answer the following questions.

1. **Inferring** What is the purpose of this investigation?

_____

_____

_____

2. **Calculating** To prepare for this calculation, solve for x in the following proportion problems.

a. $\dfrac{x}{5} = \dfrac{100,000}{20}$

_____

b. $\dfrac{x}{5} = \dfrac{200,000}{50}$

_____

3. Inferring Why is it important to never look directly at the sun?

_____

_____

_____

4. Applying Concepts How are the cards used in this investigation? How are the cards and the proportional relationships useful for determining the diameter of the sun?

_____

_____

_____

5. Predicting Do you think your calculation of the sun's diameter will be completely accurate? Explain your answer.

_____

_____

_____

Materials *(per group)*

2 index cards (10 cm × 15 cm)

metric ruler

drawing compass

tape

meter stick

scissors

Safety 🥽 ✂️ ⚠️

Be careful when handling sharp instruments. **CAUTION:** *Never look directly at the sun.* Note all safety symbols next to the steps in the Procedure and review the meaning of each symbol by referring to the symbol guide on page xiii.

Procedure

Part A: Measuring Distances and Calculating Ratios

1. Measure the base of each of the two triangles in Figure 1. Record your measurements in Data Table 1.

2. Measure the altitude (distance from tip to base) of each of the two triangles in Figure 1. Record your measurements in Data Table 1.

3. Determine the ratio between the base of the large triangle and the base of the small triangle. Record this ratio in Data Table 1.

4. Determine the ratio between the altitude of Triangle 1 and the altitude of Triangle 2. Record this ratio in Data Table 1.

5. Think about how these two ratios compare. In Part B of this lab, you will use a similar procedure to determine the diameter of the sun.

   - The base of Triangle 2 will represent the diameter of the image of the sun on a card.

   - The altitude of Triangle 2 will represent the distance between the two cards in the device you will construct.

   - The altitude of Triangle 1 will represent the distance from Earth to the sun.

   - The base of Triangle 1 will represent the diameter of the sun, which you will determine.

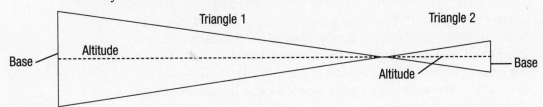

Figure 1

Part B: Determining the Diameter of the Sun

6. Using the scissors, cut I-shaped slits in each card in the positions shown in Figure 2. The meter stick should be able to slide through the slits, but the slits should be small enough so that the meter stick fits snugly. **CAUTION:** *Be careful when handling sharp instruments.*

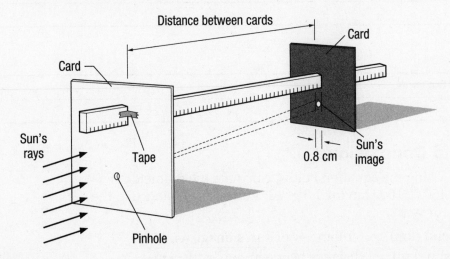

Figure 2

7. With the tip of the compass, punch a round pinhole in one of the cards in the position shown in Figure 2. Tape this card to the meter stick at the 5-cm mark so that it is perpendicular to the meter stick. **CAUTION:** *Be careful when handling sharp instruments.*

8. On the other card, draw two parallel lines exactly 0.8 cm (8 mm) apart directly below the slit, as shown in Figure 2. Slide this card onto the meter stick. Do not tape this card to the meter stick.

9. While outdoors on a sunny day, position the meter stick so that the taped card is directly facing the sun. Position the meter stick until it casts a shadow over the movable card. **CAUTION:** *Never look directly at the sun.*

10. You should be able to see a circle of light on the movable card caused by the sun's rays passing through the pinhole on the first card. If you do not see the circle of light, continue to adjust the position of the meter stick until you see the circle.

11. The circle of light on the second card is an image of the sun. Slide the movable card until the image of the sun fits exactly between the two parallel lines you drew earlier.

12. Make sure that both cards are perpendicular to the meter stick. You will know they are perpendicular when the circle of light, the sun's image, is brightest and sharpest and as close to a circle as possible. Tape the second card in place. Measure the distance between the two cards. Record your measurement in Data Table 2.

Observations

DATA TABLE 1

	Base	Altitude
Triangle 1 (large triangle)		
Triangle 2 (small triangle)		
Ratio (large:small)		

DATA TABLE 2

Distance between two cards	
Diameter of sun's image	

Analysis and Conclusions

1. **Calculating** Using the equation below, calculate the diameter of the sun. Use 150,000,000 km (or 1.5×10^8 km) as the distance to the sun. Show your work.

$$\frac{\text{diameter of sun (km)}}{\text{distance to sun (km)}} = \frac{\text{diameter of sun's image (cm)}}{\text{distance between two cards (cm)}}$$

Name _____ Class _____ Date _____

2. **Calculating** The actual diameter of the sun is 1,391,000 km. Using the equation below, determine the percentage error in your calculated value for the sun's diameter. Show your work.

$$\text{percentage error} = \frac{\text{difference between your value and the correct value}}{\text{correct value}} \times 100$$

3. **Analyzing Data** What could account for the difference in your calculation of the sun's diameter and the actual diameter of the sun?

_____

_____

_____

_____

_____

_____

4. **Applying Concepts** How might the technique used in this investigation be useful in making other astronomical measurements?

_____

_____

_____

5. **Relating Cause and Effect** How might clouds in the sky affect the accuracy of your measurement in this investigation?

_____

_____

_____

_____

Go Further

A sunspot moves along the sun's equator. If the sunspot takes 12.5 days to move from one side of the sun to the other, use the steps below to calculate how fast the sunspot is moving.

1. Using the actual value for the diameter of the sun and the formula below, calculate the circumference of the sun. The value of π (pi) is approximately 3.14.

   circumference = π × diameter

2. The sunspot moved only halfway around the sun, so to calculate the distance it traveled in 12.5 days, divide the value for the circumference by 2.

3. To calculate the distance traveled by the sunspot in one day, divide the distance you calculated in Step 2 by 12.5.

4. Explain why this value is also the speed at which the sun's surface is moving at the equator.

   _____

   _____

   _____

Modeling the Rotation
of Neutron Stars

Introduction

Any spinning object will spin faster if it contracts. This concept is
called **conservation of angular momentum.** You can see it in action
when figure skaters execute spins. They slowly pull in their arms to
make themselves twirl faster and faster. By pulling in their arms, they
pull their mass closer to their rotational axis.

The same thing happens to stars when they collapse. During a
supernova, the core of a star collapses into a very hot neutron star
about 20 km in diameter. Some of the star's mass is lost in the
explosion, but the mass that remains is tightly compressed around the
rotational axis. As the star collapses, it will rotate faster for the same
reason ice skaters rotate faster as they pull in their arms. The
collapsing star can rotate at a speed of up to 1000 rotations per second.

In this investigation, you will use a rotating square of cardboard
and masses to model the effects of mass contraction on rates of
rotation.

Problem

What causes neutron stars to rotate so rapidly?

Pre-Lab Discussion

*Read the entire investigation. Then work with a partner to answer the
following questions.*

1. **Formulating Hypotheses** Write a hypothesis that states what you
   expect will happen to the rate of spin when you decrease the
   distance between the masses on the cardboard square.

   _____

   _____

   _____

2. **Controlling Variables** What is the independent variable in this
   investigation?

   _____

3. **Controlling Variables** What is the dependent variable in this
   investigation?

   _____

4. Observing After a supergiant becomes a neutron star, what is its comparative size and mass? What happens to its rotation speed?

_____

_____

_____

5. Inferring How will this investigation help to answer the question of why neutron stars rotate so rapidly?

_____

_____

_____

_____

Materials *(per group)*
pencil with eraser
square of stiff cardboard, at least 35 cm wide
pushpin
masking tape
large, metal knitting needle
2 identical small masses
metric ruler
clock or watch with second hand

Safety 🥽 ✂️ ⚠️
Put on safety goggles. Be careful when handling sharp objects. Make sure that your weights are securely attached so they will not fly off and hit anyone. Note all safety alert symbols next to the steps in the Procedure and review the meaning of each symbol by referring to the Safety Symbols on page xiii.

Procedure
✂️ 1. Draw lines along the two diagonals of the cardboard square, as shown in Figure 1. Punch a hole through the center of the cardboard with the pushpin. **CAUTION:** *Be careful when handling sharp objects.*

2. Push the pushpin through the cardboard and into the eraser end of the pencil. The cardboard should spin freely. If it sticks, use the pushpin to widen the hole.

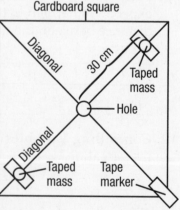

Figure1

3. Attach a piece of masking tape to one corner of the square to serve as a marker. Measure 30 cm from the center of the cardboard to the corner and use masking tape to attach one of the masses, as shown in Figure 1. Measure 30 cm from the center to the other corner and use masking tape to attach the other mass. The masses should both lie along one of the two diagonals that pass through the center. The card will be balanced because the masses are the same distance from the center.

4. Hold the pencil in front of you and perpendicular to your body so that the square of cardboard rotates below eye level and parallel to your body. Try to give each spin of the square the same force. **CAUTION:** *Make sure that masses stay attached and do not fly off and hit anyone.*

5. Spin the square. Watch the taped corner as it goes by and count the number of times it passes in 5 seconds. If the square slows down during this time, adjust the pushpin so that it turns with less friction. Record the number of rotations in the Data Table.

6. Move the masses inward toward the center so that each is 20 cm from the center and tape them down. Spin the cardboard and count the number of rotations in 5 seconds. Make sure that you apply the same force you did before. Record the number of rotations in the Data Table.

7. Repeat Step 6, but tape the masses so that each is only 10 cm from the center. Record the number of rotations in 5 seconds in the Data Table.

Observations

DATA TABLE

Distance of Masses from Center of Square	Number of Rotations (spins)
30 cm	
20 cm	
10 cm	

Analysis and Conclusions

1. Calculate Calculate the rotation rate for each trial by dividing the number of spins by 5 seconds.

2. Making Judgments Did any unexpected variable seem to affect the outcome of your investigation?

_____

_____

_____

3. Inferring Why was it important that the masses were the same distance from the axis for each trial?

_____

_____

_____

4. **Infer** Explain why the rate of rotation of a neutron star is so great compared to that of the star from which it formed.

_____

_____

_____

5. **Evaluating and Revising** How could you improve this model to more accurately represent the concept of conservation of angular momentum as it pertains to neutron stars?

_____

_____

_____

_____

_____

_____

Go Further

What happens to the rotation rate when mass decreases? Repeat Step 6 two more times, but for the first trial, use masses that are about one-half the mass of the initial masses used. For the second trial, use masses that are one-fourth the mass of the initial masses used. Create a data table in which to record your results.

Determining Latitude and Longitude

Using maps and globes to find places and features on Earth's surface is an essential skill required of all Earth scientists. The grid that is formed by lines of latitude and longitude form the basis for locating points on Earth. Latitude lines indicate north-south distance, and longitude lines indicate east-west distance. Degrees are used to mark latitude and longitude distances on Earth's surface. Degrees can be divided into sixty equal parts called minutes ('), and a minute of angle can be divided into sixty parts called seconds ("). Thus, 31°10'20" means 31 degrees, 10 minutes, and 20 seconds. This exercise will introduce you to the systems used for determining location on Earth.

Problem How are latitude and longitude calculated, and how do they indicate a particular location on the globe?

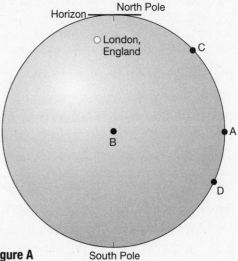

Figure A

Materials
- globe
- protractor
- ruler
- world map

Skills Interpreting, Measuring, Inferring

Procedure

Part A: Determining Latitude

1. Figure A represents Earth, with point B its center. Locate the equator on the globe. Sketch and label the equator on Figure A. Label the Northern Hemisphere and Southern Hemisphere on Figure A.

2. On Figure A, make an angle by drawing a line from point A on the equator to point B (the center of Earth). Then extend the line from point B to point C in the Northern Hemisphere. The angle you have drawn (∠ABC) is 45°. By definition of latitude, point C is located at 45°N latitude.

3. Draw a line on Figure A through point C that is also parallel to the equator. What is the latitude at all points on this line? Record this number on the line you draw.

4. Draw a line on Figure A from point D to point B. Using a protractor, measure ∠ABD on your paper. Then draw a line parallel to the equator that also goes through point D. Label the line with its proper latitude.

5. How many degrees of latitude separate the latitude lines (or parallels) on the globe that you are using? Record the degrees of latitude.

6. Refer to Figure B. Determine the latitude for each point A–F. Be sure to indicate whether it is north or south of the equator and include the word "latitude." Record these numbers.

_____

_____

7. Use a globe or map to locate the cities listed below. Record their latitude to the nearest degree.

   A. Moscow, Russia _____

   B. Durban, South Africa _____

   C. Your home city _____

8. Use the globe or map to find the name of a city or feature that is equally as far south of the equator as your home city is north.

_____

Part B: Determining Longitude

9. Locate the prime meridian on Figure C. Sketch and label the prime meridian on Figure C. Label the Eastern and Western Hemispheres.

10. How many degrees of longitude separate each meridian on your globe?

_____

11. Refer to Figure C. Determine the longitude for each point A–F. Be sure to indicate whether it is east or west of the prime meridian.

_____

12. Use the globe or map to give the name of a city or feature that is equally as far east of the prime meridian as your home city is west.

_____

Analyze and Conclude

1. **Applying Concepts** What is the maximum number of 1 degree longitude or latitude lines that can be drawn on a globe?

_____

2. **Comparing and Contrasting** Why do longitude lines converge while latitude lines do not?

_____

_____

_____

3. **Thinking Critically** Amelia Earhart, her flight engineer, and her
   plane are believed to have been lost somewhere over the Pacific
   Ocean. It is now thought that the coordinates that she was given
   for her fuel stop at Howley Island in the Pacific Ocean were
   wrong. Knowing what you do about how latitude and longitude
   coordinates are written, why would a wrong number have been
   so catastrophic for her?

   _____

   _____

   _____

   _____

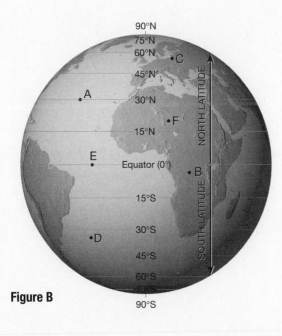

Figure B

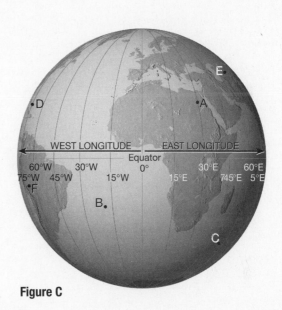

Figure C

Mineral Identification

Most minerals can be easily identified by using the properties discussed in this chapter. In this lab, you will use what you have learned about mineral properties and the table in the DataBank to identify some common rock-forming minerals. In Chapter 3, you will learn about rocks, which are mixtures of one or more minerals. Being able to identify minerals will enable you to understand more about the processes that form and change the rocks at and beneath Earth's surface.

Problem How can you use simple tests and tools to identify common minerals?

Materials
- mineral samples
- hand lens
- streak plate
- copper penny
- steel knife blade
- glass plate
- piece of quartz
- dilute hydrochloric acid
- magnet
- hammer
- 50-mL graduated cylinder
- tap water
- balance
- thin thread
- scissors
- paper or cloth towels
- Resource 16 in the DataBank

Skills Observing, Comparing and Contrasting, Measuring

Procedure 🖐️📋📑📋🔪🔍📋

Part A: Color and Luster

1. Examine each mineral sample with and without the hand lens. Examine both the central part of each mineral as well as the edges of the samples.

2. Record the color and luster of each sample in the Data Table.

DATA TABLE

Mineral Number	Color	Luster	Streak	Relative Hardness	Cleavage/ Fracture	Density m	V_1	V_2	d	Other Properties
1										
2										
3										
4										
5										
6										
7										
8										

Part B: Streak and Hardness

3. To determine the streak of a mineral, gently drag it across the streak plate and observe the color of the powdered mineral. If a mineral is harder than the streak plate (H = 7), it will not produce a streak.

Name _____ Class _____ Date _____

4. Record the streak color for each mineral in the Data Table.

5. Use your fingernail, the penny, the glass plate, the knife blade, and the piece of quartz to test the hardness of each mineral. Remember that if a mineral scratches an object, the mineral is harder than the object. If an object scratches a mineral, the mineral is softer than the object.

6. Record the hardness values for each sample in the Data Table.

Part C: Cleavage and Fracture

7. Gently strike one of the mineral samples with a hammer. **CAUTION:** *Be sure to put on your goggles. Make sure that everyone is out of the way of flying pieces.*

8. Observe the broken mineral pieces. Does the mineral cleave or fracture? Remember that cleavage is breakage along flat, even surfaces, and fracture is uneven breakage. Record your observations in the Data Table.

9. Repeat Steps 7 and 8 for the other minerals. Record your observations for each mineral in the Data Table.

Part D: Density

10. Using a balance, determine the mass of your mineral samples. Record the mass in the first column (*m*) under Density.

11. Cut a piece of thread about 20 cm long. Tie a small piece of one mineral sample to one end of the thread.

12. Securely tie the other end of the thread to a pencil or pen.

13. Fill the graduated cylinder about half-full with water. Record the exact volume of the water in the second column (V_1) under Density.

14. Lower the mineral into the graduated cylinder. Read the volume of the water. Record the volume in the third column (V_2).

15. Calculate the density of the mineral using the following equation:

$$\frac{\text{mass}_1}{\text{volume}_2 - \text{volume}_1}$$

Record this value in the fourth column (*d*). Repeat Steps 10–15 for the other minerals. Record the densities in the Data Table.

Part E: Other Properties

16. Use the magnet to determine if any of the minerals are magnetic. Record your observations in the Data Table under Other Properties.

17. Place the transparent minerals over a word on this page to see if any have the property of double refraction. If a mineral has this property, you will see two sets of the word. Record your observations in the last column under Other Properties.

18. Compare the feel of the minerals. In the Data Table, note any differences in the last column.

Earth Science Lab Manual ▪ **166**

© Pearson Education, Inc., publishing as Pearson Prentice Hall. All rights reserved.

19. Carefully place one or two drops of dilute hydrochloric acid on each mineral. Record your observations in the last column. When you are finished with this test, wash the minerals well with tap water to rinse away the acid. **CAUTION:** *Always be careful when working with acids.*

Analyze and Conclude

1. **Identifying** Use the data and Resource 16 in the DataBank to identify each of the minerals tested.

_____

_____

2. **Evaluating** Which of the properties did you find most useful? Least useful? Give reasons for your answers.

_____

_____

_____

3. **Comparing and Contrasting** In general, how did the minerals with metallic luster differ from those with nonmetallic luster?

_____

_____

4. **Classifying** Classify your minerals into at least three groups based on your observations. How does your classification scheme differ from those of at least two other students?

_____

_____

_____

Rock Identification

Most rocks can be easily identified by texture and composition. In this lab, you will use what you have learned about rocks as well as the information on minerals from Chapter 2 to identify some common rocks.

Problem How can you use composition and texture to identify common rocks?

Materials
- rock samples
- hand lens
- pocket knife
- dilute hydrochloric acid
- colored pencils
- Resources 16 and 17 in the DataBank

Skills Observing, Comparing and Contrasting, Measuring

Procedure 🔥🧤🧪👁🧥

1. Use the Data Table to record your observations. Add any other columns that you think might be useful.

2. Examine each rock specimen with and without the hand lens. Determine and record the overall color of each rock in the Data Table.

3. Try to identify all of the minerals in each rock, using the information in Resources 16 and 17 in the DataBank. Record your observations in the Data Table.

4. Determine and record the presence of any organic matter in any of the samples.

5. Observe the relationships among the minerals in each rock to determine texture. Refer to Resources 16 and 17 in the DataBank if necessary. Record your observations.

👁🧤 6. Note and record any other unique observations of the samples. **CAUTION:** *Always be careful when working with acids.*

7. In the Data Table, make and color a detailed sketch of each sample.

8. Identify each sample as being an igneous rock, a sedimentary rock, or a metamorphic rock.

9. Name each sample. Use the photographs in this chapter and Resources 16 and 17 in the DataBank if necessary.

DATA TABLE

Rock Number	Overall Color	Composition	Texture	Sketch	Rock Type	Rock Name
1.						
2.						
3.						
4.						
5.						

Analyze and Conclude

1. **Evaluating** Which of the rock identification characteristics did you find most useful? Which of the characteristics did you find least useful? Give reasons for your answers.

_____

_____

2. **Comparing and Contrasting** How did identifying rocks compare with the mineral identification lab you did in Chapter 2? How is identifying rocks different from identifying the minerals that compose the rocks?

_____

_____

_____

3. **Applying Concepts** Match the metamorphic rocks with their probable parent rocks.

_____

_____

_____

4. **Applying Concepts** Choose two pairs of rocks used in this investigation. Write a brief description for each pair that explains how one rock can be changed into the other. Refer to the diagram of the rock cycle in Chapter 3.

_____

_____

Finding the Product that Best Conserves Resources

When you buy a product, you usually consider factors such as price, brand name, quality, and quantity. But do you consider the amount of resources the package uses? Many products come in packages of different types and materials. You might buy a larger pack if you use a lot, or a tiny pack if you like the convenience of individual servings. But how much cardboard, plastic, or glass are you using—or wasting—depending on your choice? How about the trees, petroleum, and other resources needed to make those packages? In this lab, you will compare three sets of packages that hold the same amount of juice to determine how your decisions about packaging affect the use of resources.

Problem Which packaging conserves resources the best?

Materials

- 1 1.89-L (64-fl. oz) cardboard juice carton
- 1 946-mL (32-fl. oz) cardboard juice carton
- 1 240-mL (8-fl. oz) cardboard juice carton
- scissors
- metric ruler

CAUTION: *Be careful when using scissors.*

Skills Observing, Measuring, Calculating, Comparing and Contrasting, Relating Cause and Effect, Drawing Conclusions

Procedure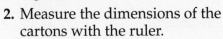

Part A: Determine the Amount of Material in Each Package

1. Work in groups of three or four. Use scissors to cut apart the three cartons your teacher gives your group. Then spread each one out as you see in Figure 1.

2. Measure the dimensions of the cartons with the ruler.

3. Calculate the area of each carton. Use these equations:

   - Area of a rectangle:
     $A = l \times w$
     (l = length; w = width)

   - Area of a square:
     $A = s^2$
     (s = length of a side of the square)

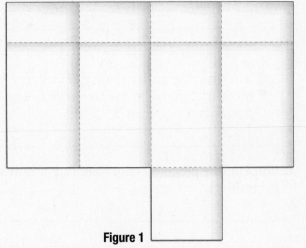

Figure 1

_____

_____

_____

Name _____ Class _____ Date _____

4. Record the data you calculated in the Data Table.

DATA TABLE

	Amount of Cardboard in One Carton	Number of Cartons Needed to Hold 1.89 L	Amount of Cardboard Needed to Hold 1.89 L
1.89 L		1	
946 mL		2	
240 mL		8	

Part B: Compare the Area of Material in the Packages

5. Calculate how much more cardboard is used when you buy 1.89 L of juice in the two 946-mL cartons instead of one 1.89-L carton.

Use this procedure:

a.) Subtract the area of material in the 1.89-L carton from the area of material in the two 946-mL cartons.

_____

_____

b.) Divide the answer you get in Part A by the area of material in the 1.89-L carton.

_____

_____

c.) Multiply the answer you get in Part B by 100. This is how much more material is in the two containers, expressed as a percentage.

_____

6. Repeat this procedure for the area of material in eight small containers.

_____

_____

_____

_____

_____

Analyze and Conclude

1. **Comparing and Contrasting** Based on your data, does buying the juice in one large carton or in an eight-pack of small individual cartons use more cardboard? How does buying the juice in two medium-sized cartons compare?

_____

_____

_____

2. **Relating Cause and Effect** How does buying the juice in several cartons instead of one large carton impact the use of resources?

_____

_____

3. **Drawing Conclusions** Suppose you have determined which set of cardboard cartons uses the least resources. Then you find out that the same size carton of juice comes in plastic and glass as well as cardboard. How would you decide which of these containers would be the best choice, in terms of saving resources?

_____

_____

_____

_____

_____

_____

Chapter 5   Weathering, Soil, and Mass Movements   **Exploration Lab**

Effect of Temperature on Chemical Weathering

Water is the most important agent of chemical weathering. One way water promotes chemical weathering is by dissolving the minerals in rocks. In this lab, you will model the effect of temperature on chemical weathering by measuring the rate at which antacid tablets dissolve in water at different temperatures. These tablets contain calcium carbonate, the mineral found in rocks such as limestone and marble.

Problem How does temperature affect the rate of chemical weathering?

Materials

- 250-mL beaker
- thermometer
- hot water (40–50°C)
- ice
- 5 antacid tablets
- stopwatch

Skills Measuring, Using Tables and Graphs, Drawing Conclusions, Inferring

Procedure 🔥 💧 🧍

1. Use the Data Table to record your measurements.

2. Add a mixture of hot water and ice to the beaker. Use the thermometer to measure the temperature of the mixture. Add either more hot water or more ice until the temperature is between 0°C and 10°C. The total volume of the mixture should be about 200 mL.

3. When the temperature is within the correct range, remove any remaining ice from the beaker. Record the starting temperature of the water in the Data Table. Remove the thermometer from the beaker.

4. Drop an antacid tablet into the beaker. Start the stopwatch as soon as the tablet enters the water. Stop the stopwatch when the tablet has completely dissolved and no traces of the tablet are visible. (Don't wait for the bubbling to stop.) Record the time in the Data Table.

5. Place the thermometer in the beaker and wait for the temperature of the water to stabilize. Record the final temperature of the water in the Data Table.

6. Calculate the average temperature by adding the starting and final temperatures and dividing by 2. Record the result in the Data Table.

7. Repeat Steps 2–6 four more times, once at each of the following temperature ranges: 10–20°C, 20–30°C, 30–40°C, and 40–50°C. Adjust the relative amounts of hot water and ice to produce the correct water temperatures. The total volume of water and ice should always be about 200 mL.

Name _____ Class _____ Date _____

8. On the following graph, add labels for temperature ranges and time intervals. Then plot your data on the graph. Draw a smooth curve through the data points.

DATA TABLE

Starting Temperature (°C)	Dissolving Time (s)	Final Temperature (°C)	Average Temperature (°C)

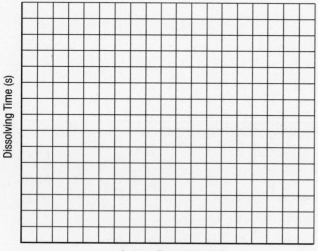

Average Temperature (ºC)

Analyze and Conclude

1. Analyzing Data At which temperature did the antacid tablet dissolve most rapidly?

_____

2. Analyzing Data At which temperature did the antacid tablet dissolve most slowly?

_____

3. Drawing Conclusions What is the relationship between temperature and the rate at which antacid tablets dissolve in water?

_____

4. Formulating Hypotheses Based on your observations, form a hypothesis about the relationship between temperature and the rate of chemical weathering.

_____

5. Designing Experiments How could you test your hypothesis?

_____

_____

_____

6. Predicting What would your results have been if you had ground each tablet into a fine powder before dropping it into the water? Would your conclusion be the same or different? Explain.

_____

_____

_____

_____

7. Inferring Would a limestone building weather more rapidly in Homer, Alaska, or in Honolulu, Hawaii? (Both cities receive about the same amount of precipitation in an average year.) Explain your reasoning.

_____

_____

_____

_____

8. Communicating Write a lab report in which you explain your procedures in this lab and discuss whether or not your data supported your hypothesis. In your report, identify the manipulated variable and the responding variable in this experiment.

_____

_____

_____

Name _____ Class _____ Date _____

Chapter 6   Running Water and Groundwater   **Exploration Lab**

Investigating the Permeability of Soils

The permeability of soils affects the way groundwater moves—or if it moves at all. Some soils are highly permeable, while others are not. In this lab, you will determine the permeability of various soils, and draw conclusions about their effect on the movement of water underground.

Problem How does the permeability of soil affect its ability to move water?

Materials

- 100-mL graduated cylinder
- beaker
- small funnel
- 3 pieces of cotton
- samples of coarse sand, fine sand, and soil
- clock or watch with a second hand

Skills Observing, Measuring, Comparing and Contrasting, Analyzing Data, Interpreting Data

Procedure 🦾 🖐

1. Place a small, clean piece of cotton in the neck of the funnel. Fill the funnel above the cotton with coarse sand. Fill the funnel about two-thirds of the way.

2. Pour water into the graduated cylinder until it reaches the 50-mL mark.

3. With the bottom of the funnel over the beaker, pour the water from the graduated cylinder slowly into the sand in the funnel.

4. In the Data Table, keep track of the time from the second you start to pour the water into the funnel. Measure the amount of time that it takes the water to drain through the funnel filled with coarse sand. Using the graduated cylinder, measure the amount of water recovered in the beaker.

5. Record in the Data Table the time it takes for the water to drain through the sand.

6. Empty and clean the measuring cylinder, funnel, and beaker.

7. Repeat Steps 1 through 7, first using fine sand, and then using soil.

DATA TABLE

	Time Needed for Water to Drain Through Funnel	Water Collected in Beaker (mL)
Coarse sand		
Fine sand		
Soil		

Analyze and Conclude

1. **Comparing and Contrasting** Of the three materials you tested, which has the greatest permeability? Which had the least permeability?

   _____

   _____

   _____

2. **Analyzing Data** Why were different amounts of water recovered in the beaker for each material tested?

   _____

   _____

   _____

3. **Interpreting Data** What effect would the differences you observed in this lab have on the movement of groundwater through different soils?

   _____

   _____

   _____

4. **Controlling Variables** What factors might affect the accuracy of your results in this experiment? How would repeating each test several times affect your measurements?

   _____

   _____

   _____

Interpreting a Glacial Landscape

Topographic maps are valuable tools geologists use to interpret landscapes. Especially in the field—when your view can be limited—these maps not only help you determine your location, they can offer a bigger landscape picture than what is actually visible. See how well you can identify glacial features on the map and interpret them to reconstruct geologic history.

Problem How can a topographic map allow you to interpret a glacially formed landscape?

Materials
- Resource 23 in the DataBank
- piece of blank paper

Skills Graphing, Inferring, Drawing Conclusions

Procedure

1. Following line A on the map, sketch a topographic profile of the Lake Fork Valley onto the Topographic Profile sheet on the next page. Place the straight edge of your blank paper along the line and mark in pencil where it meets every fifth contour line (the darker guide contours). Be sure to write the elevation of every fifth contour line along the *y*-axis of the Topographic Profile sheet.

2. How can you tell from your profile that the valley was formed by a glacier?

_____

3. Was the valley shaped by a continental ice sheet or by a valley glacier? Explain how you know.

_____

_____

4. Use the map to help you describe the direction the glacier flowed through this valley. How can you tell?

_____

5. Which letter arrow points to cirques? You can refer to Figure 7 in your textbook for help.

_____

6. The lakes inside cirques are called tarns. Identify the tarns inside the cirques you just found.

_____

7. Which letter arrows point to hanging valleys?

_____

8. Which letter arrows point to arêtes?

_____

9. Name a peak on the map that is a horn.

_____

10. Feature E on the map is composed of glacial till. What type of glacial feature is E, and how did it form?

_____

_____

11. Explain how Turquoise Lake formed.

_____

_____

_____

_____

_____

SOUTH   NORTH

Sugar Loaf Mountain   Bear Lake

Topographic Profile sheet

Chapter 8   Earthquakes and Earth's Interior

Locating an Earthquake

The focus of an earthquake is the actual place within Earth where the earthquake originates. When locating an earthquake on a map, scientists plot the epicenter, the point on Earth's surface directly above the focus. To locate an epicenter, records from three different seismographs are needed.

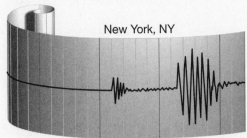

New York, NY

9:00 UTC (Time marks in minutes)

Problem How can you determine the location of an earthquake's epicenter?

Materials

- drawing compass
- world map or atlas

Skills Measuring, Interpreting Maps, Interpreting Graphs

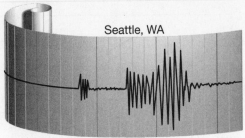

Seattle, WA

9:00 UTC

Procedure 🖉🔧

1. The seismograms shown in Figure 1 recorded the same earthquake. Use the Travel-Time Graph to determine the distance of each station from the epicenter. Record your answers in the Data Table.

2. Refer to a world map or atlas for the locations of the three seismic stations. Place a small dot showing the location of each of the three stations on the map in Figure 2. Neatly label each city on the map.

Mexico City, Mexico

9:00 UTC

Figure 1

3. On the map in Figure 2, use a drawing compass to draw a circle around each of the three stations. The radius of the circle, in miles, should be equal to each station's distance from the epicenter. Use the scale on the map to set the distance on the drawing compass for each station. **CAUTION:** *Use care when handling the drawing compass.*

DATA TABLE

	New York	**Seattle**	**Mexico City**
Elapsed time between first P and first S waves			
Distance from epicenter in miles			

Analyze and Conclude

1. Using Graphs How far from the epicenter are the three cities located?

_____

_____

_____

2. Calculating What would the distances from the epicenter to the cities be in kilometers?

_____

_____

_____

3. Interpreting Maps What is the approximate latitude and longitude of the epicenter of the earthquake that was recorded by the three stations? Use the map in Figure 3.

_____

4. Drawing Conclusions On the New York seismogram, the first P wave was recorded at 9:01 UTC. UTC is the international standard on which most countries base their time. At what time (UTC) did the earthquake actually occur? Explain.

_____

_____

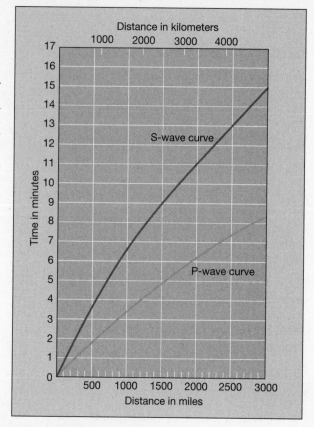

Figure 2 Travel-Time Graph

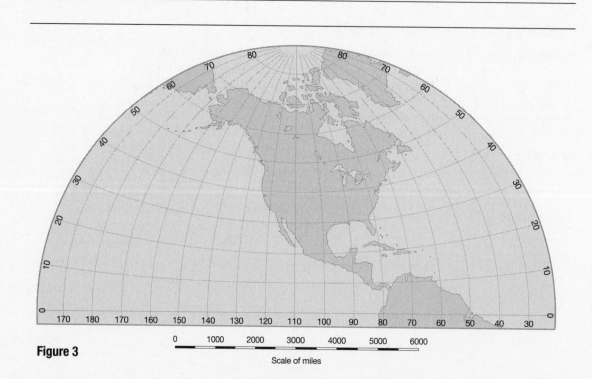

Figure 3

Scale of miles

Paleomagnetism and the Ocean Floor

When Wegener proposed his hypothesis of continental drift, little was known about the ocean floor. He thought that the continents plowed through the ocean floor like icebreaking ships plowing through ice. Later studies of the oceans provided one of the keys to the plate tectonic theory. In this lab, you will observe how the magnetic rocks on the ocean floor can be used to understand plate tectonics.

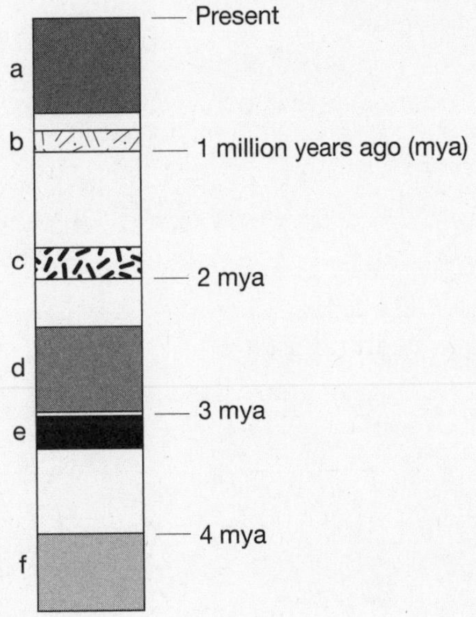

Problem How are the paleomagnetic patterns on the ocean floor used to determine the rate of seafloor spreading?

Materials
- metric ruler
- calculator

Figure 1

Skills Measuring, Interpreting Diagrams, Calculating

Procedure
1. Scientists have reconstructed Earth's magnetic polarity reversals over the past several million years. A record of these reversals is shown in Figure 1. Periods of normal polarity, when a compass would have pointed north as it does today, are shown in grayscale. Periods of reverse polarity are shown in white. Record the number of times Earth's magnetic field has had reversed polarity in the last 4 million years.

_____

2. The three diagrams in Figure 2 on the next page illustrate the magnetic polarity reversals across sections of the mid-ocean ridges in the Pacific, South Atlantic, and North Atlantic oceans. Periods of normal polarity are shown in the same grayscale in the illustration above. Observe that the patterns of polarity in the rock match on either side of the ridge for each ocean basin.

3. On the three ocean-floor diagrams, identify and mark the periods of normal polarity with the letters *a–f*. Begin at the rift valley and label along both sides of each ridge. (*Hint:* The left side of the South Atlantic has already been done and can act as a guide.)

4. Using the South Atlantic as an example, label the beginning of the normal polarity period c, "2 million years ago," on the left sides of the Pacific and North Atlantic diagrams.

Name _____ Class _____ Date _____

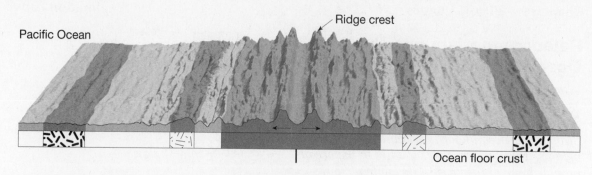

Pacific Ocean

Ridge crest

Ocean floor crust

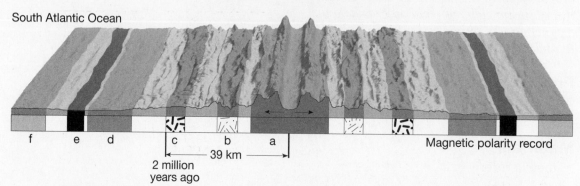

South Atlantic Ocean

f   e   d   c   b   a

|← 39 km →|

2 million
years ago

Magnetic polarity record

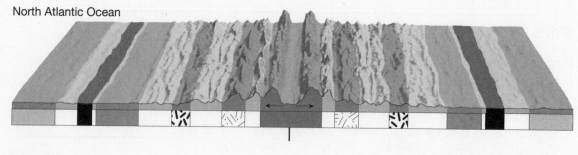

North Atlantic Ocean

Figure 2

0   20   40 km

Scale

5. Using the distance scale shown with the ocean floor diagrams, determine which ocean basin has spread the greatest distance during the last 2 million years. (Measure from the center of the rift valley.)

_____

_____

6. Refer to the distance scale. Notice that the left side of the South Atlantic basin has spread approximately 39 kilometers from the center of the rift valley in 2 million years.

Analyze and Conclude

1. **Analyzing Data** How many kilometers has the left side of the Pacific basin spread in 2 million years?

_____

2. Analyzing Data How many kilometers has the left side of the North Atlantic basin spread in 2 million years?

_____

_____

3. Inferring How many kilometers has each ocean basin opened in the past 2 million years?

_____

_____

4. Calculating If both the distance that each ocean basin has opened and the time it took to open that distance are known, the rate of seafloor spreading can be calculated. Determine the rate of seafloor spreading for the South Atlantic Ocean basin in centimeters per year. (*Hint:* To determine the rate of spreading in centimeters per year for each ocean basin, first convert the distance from kilometers to centimeters and then divide this distance by the time, 2 million years.)

_____

_____

5. Calculating Determine the rate of seafloor spreading for the North Atlantic and Pacific Ocean basins.

_____

_____

6. Drawing Conclusions Which ocean basin is spreading the fastest? The slowest?

_____

_____

7. Inferring Do ocean basins spread uniformly over the entire basin? Explain.

_____

_____

_____

Chapter 11   Mountain Building

Investigating Anticlines and Synclines

The axial plane of a fold is an imaginary plane drawn through the long axis of a fold. The axial plane divides the fold into two halves called limbs as shown in Figure 1. In a symmetrical fold, the limbs are mirror images of each other and move away at the same angle. In an asymmetrical fold, the limbs dip or tilt at different angles. Folds do not continue forever. Where folds "die out" and end, the axis is no longer horizontal, and the fold is said to be plunging, as shown in Figure 2. A geologic principle known as the principle of superposition states that in most situations with layered rocks, the oldest rocks are at the bottom of the sequence.

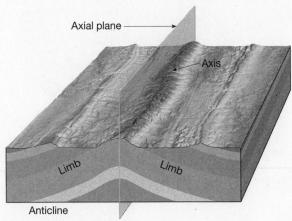

Figure 1 Horizontal Axis

Problem How are rocks oriented in anticlines and synclines?

Materials
• protractor

Skills Observing, Measuring, Classifying, Interpreting Diagrams

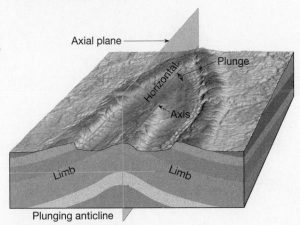

Figure 2 Plunging Axis

Procedure

1. Study the two diagrams, labeled Fold A and Fold B in Figures 3 and 4.

2. Use a protractor to measure the angles of the rock layers in both limbs of Fold A. Repeat your measurements for both limbs of Fold B. For consistency, measure the angles on both folds at the surface between layers 3 and 4. Record the measurements of the angles.

3. Use Figures 3, 4, and 5 to determine what types of folds are shown by Fold A and Fold B.

4. Anticlines and synclines are linear features caused by compressional stresses. Two other types of folds—domes and basins—are often nearly circular and result from vertical displacement. Uplift produces domes like those shown in Figure 3. A basin is a downwarped structure, as shown in Figure 4.

5. Complete the three sides of the blank block diagram on the right to show an eroded fold consistent with the rock layer shown on the right side of the block.

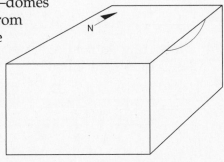

Name _____ Class _____ Date _____

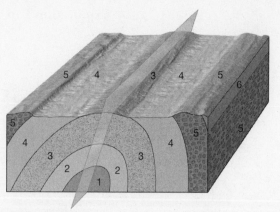

Figure 3 Fold A

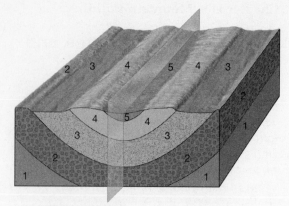

Figure 4 Fold B

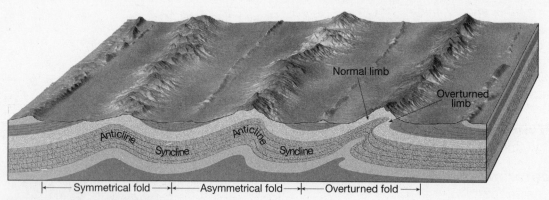

Figure 5 Anticlines and Synclines

Analyze and Conclude

1. **Interpreting Diagrams** What type of fold is shown by Fold A? In what direction do the limbs dip or tilt from the axial plane?

   _____

2. **Interpreting Diagrams** What type of fold is shown by Fold B? In what direction do the limbs dip or tilt from the axial plane?

   _____

3. **Drawing Conclusions** In Fold A, which rock layer is the oldest shown? Which rock layer is the youngest shown?

   _____

   _____

4. **Measuring** In Fold A, at what angle are the rock layers in both limbs dipping or tilted?

   _____

   _____

5. **Drawing Conclusions** In Fold B, which rock layer is the oldest shown? Which rock layer is the youngest shown?

_____

6. **Measuring** In Fold B, at what angle are the rock layers in both limbs dipping or tilted?

_____

7. **Classifying** What type of fold did you draw in the blank block diagram?

_____

8. **Observing** Is Fold A symmetrical or asymmetrical? Is Fold B symmetrical or asymmetrical?

_____

9. **Observing** Is Fold A plunging or nonplunging? Is Fold B plunging or nonplunging?

_____

10. **Applying Concepts** If you walk away from the axis on an eroded anticline, do the rocks get older or younger? How do the ages of the rocks change as you walk away from the axis in a syncline?

_____

_____

_____

Fossil Occurrence and the Age of Rocks

Groups of fossil organisms occur throughout the geologic record for specific intervals of time. This time interval is called the fossil's range. Knowing the range of the fossils of specific organisms or groups of organisms can be used to relatively date rocks and sequences of rocks. In this laboratory exercise, you will use such information to assign a date to a hypothetical unit of rock.

Problem How can the occurrence of fossils and their known age ranges be used to date rocks?

Materials
• Resource 10 in the DataBank

Skills Interpreting Diagrams, Graphing, Hypothesizing, Inferring

Procedure

1. A section of rock made up of layers of limestone and shale has been studied and samples have been taken. A large variety of fossils were collected from the rock samples. Make a bar graph using the information shown in the Data Table. Begin by listing the numbers of the individual fossils on the *x*-axis. Use the Geologic Time Scale in the DataBank to list the time units of the Geologic Time Scale on the *y*-axis.

2. Transfer the range data of each fossil onto the graph. Draw an X in each box, beginning at the oldest occurrence of the organism up to the youngest occurrence. Shade in the marked boxes. You will end up with bars depicting the geologic ranges of each of the fossils listed.

3. Examine the graph. Are there any time units that contain all of the fossils listed? Write this time period at the bottom of the graph.

DATA TABLE

	Type of Fossil	Oldest Occurrence	Youngest Occurrence
1	Foraminifera	Silurian	Quaternary
2	Bryozoan	Silurian	Permian
3	Gastropod	Devonian	Pennsylvanian
4	Brachiopod	Silurian	Mississippian
5	Bivalve	Silurian	Permian
6	Gastropod	Ordovician	Devonian
7	Trilobite	Silurian	Devonian
8	Ostracod	Devonian	Tertiary
9	Brachiopod	Cambrian	Devonian

```
            _____     ┌──┬──┬──┬──┬──┬──┐
            _____     ├──┼──┼──┼──┼──┼──┤
            _____     ├──┼──┼──┼──┼──┼──┤
            _____     ├──┼──┼──┼──┼──┼──┤
            _____     ├──┼──┼──┼──┼──┼──┤
            _____     ├──┼──┼──┼──┼──┼──┤
            _____     ├──┼──┼──┼──┼──┼──┤
            _____     ├──┼──┼──┼──┼──┼──┤
            _____     ├──┼──┼──┼──┼──┼──┤
            _____     ├──┼──┼──┼──┼──┼──┤
            _____     └──┴──┴──┴──┴──┴──┘
```

Analyze and Conclude

1. **Reading Graphs** What is the age of the hypothetical rock layer that these fossils were collected from?

   _____

   _____

2. **Inferring** Based on the age determined, do you think that this group of fossils could be considered index fossils? Why or why not?

   _____

   _____

   _____

3. **Inferring** A species of the trilobite listed in line 7 of the Data Table (*Paciphacops logani*) is limited to rocks of lower Devonian age. Trilobite fossils are widespread throughout North America. Can this fossil be considered an index fossil? Why or why not?

   _____

   _____

4. **Connecting Concepts** These fossils were collected from limestone and shale rocks. Based on what you have learned about the formation of these rock types, what type of environment did these organisms live in?

   _____

5. **Understanding Concepts** Shale often contains fossils of leaves. If the gastropods listed in line 3 and line 6 were collected from shale containing leaf fossils, could you use radiocarbon dating to assign a numerical date to this rock unit? Explain.

   _____

   _____

Chapter 13   Earth's History   **Application Lab**

Modeling the Geologic Time Scale

Applying the techniques of geologic dating, the history of Earth has been subdivided into several different units that provide a meaningful time frame. The events that make up Earth's history can be arranged within this time frame to provide a clearer picture of the past. The span of a human life is like the blink of an eye compared to the age of Earth. Because of this, it can be difficult to comprehend the magnitude of geologic time.

Problem How can the geologic time scale be represented in a way that allows a clearer visual understanding?

Materials
- strip of adding machine paper measuring 5 meters or longer
- meter stick or metric measuring tape
- Resource 10 in the DataBank

Skills Measuring, Calculating, Interpreting Diagrams

Procedure

1. Obtain a piece of adding machine paper slightly longer than 5 meters in length. Draw a line at one end of the paper and label it "Present."

2. Using the following scale, construct a timeline by completing Steps 3 and 4.

    Scale

    1 meter = 1 billion years

    10 centimeters = 100 million years

    1 centimeter = 10 million years

    1 millimeter = 1 million years

3. Using the Geologic Time Scale as a reference, divide your timeline into the eons and eras of geologic time. Label each division with its name and indicate its absolute age.

4. Using the scale, plot and label the plant and animal events on your timeline that are listed on the Geologic Time Scale.

Analyze and Conclude

1. **Calculating** What fraction or percent of geologic time is represented by the Precambrian eon?

_____

_____

2. **Explaining** Using your text and class notes as references, explain why the approximate time of 540 million years ago was selected to mark the end of the Precambrian time and the beginning of Phanerozoic eon.

_____

_____

_____

3. **Inferring** Suggest one reason why the periods of the Cenozoic era have been further subdivided into several epochs with reasonably reliable accuracy.

_____

_____

_____

_____

4. **Analyzing Data** How many times longer is the whole of geologic time than the time represented by the 5000 years of recorded history?

_____

_____

_____

5. **Calculating** For what fraction or percent of geologic time have land plants been present on Earth?

_____

_____

_____

Modeling Seafloor Depth Transects

Oceanographers use a number of methods to determine the depth and topography of the ocean floor. Technology—such as sonar, satellites, and submersibles—has allowed scientists to produce detailed maps of the ocean floor in each ocean basin. In this lab, you will model a seafloor depth transect to determine the topography of an ocean basin created by your classmates.

Problem How can the topography of an ocean basin be determined?

Materials

- shoe box
- modeling clay
- aluminum foil
- metric ruler
- scalpel
- Resource 18 in the DataBank

Skills Measuring, Graphing, Inferring, Drawing Conclusions

Procedure

Part A: Making a Model of the Seafloor

1. Examine Figures 1 and 2 and Resource 18 in the DataBank to determine which area of the ocean floor you and your group will model. Be sure to identify the specific features that would be found in the area you choose to model. For example, if you were to model the continental margin you would want to include the continental shelf, continental slope, continental rise, and some submarine canyons in your model. If you were to model the ocean basin floor, you would want to include abyssal plains, trenches, seamounts, and guyots. Do not discuss the plan for your model with students outside your group.

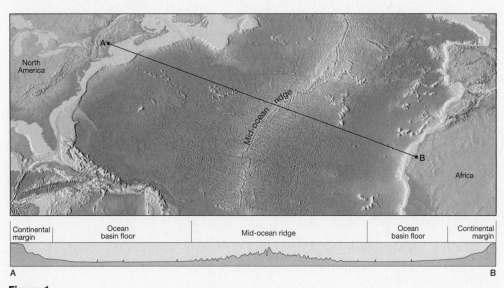

Figure 1

Name _____ Class _____ Date _____

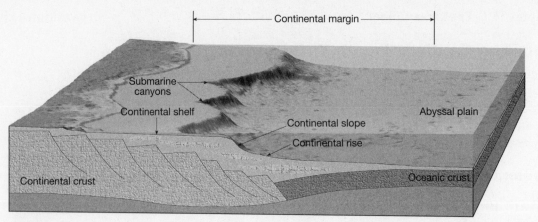

Figure 2

2. Once you have determined which area of the ocean floor you will model, use the clay to make a contoured model of the seafloor inside the shoebox.

3. Cover the box with its top and exchange boxes with another group from your class. Do not remove the top of the box that you receive from another group.

Part B: Completing a Depth Transect

4. Obtain a piece of aluminum foil that is large enough to cover the top of the shoebox and fold over the sides of the box about an inch all the way around.

5. Spread the foil flat on your lab table. Place the ruler lengthwise on the foil, parallel to the edge of the foil. The ruler can be in the middle of the foil or off to the side. The line formed by the edge of the ruler will be your transect line.

6. Use a pencil to make tick marks on the foil every centimeter along the entire length of the foil.

7. Hold the foil in place over the top of the box. Quickly and carefully remove the top of the box and set the foil piece down in place of the top. Do not look in the box. Secure the foil in place on top of the box by turning down the foil over the sides of the box. Be sure the foil is tight across the top.

8. Make tick marks along the *x*-axis of the graph once every centimeter. Make tick marks along the *y*-axis every half of a centimeter. **NOTE:** You may also use a computer to produce your graph.

9. Use the scalpel to carefully make a slit in the foil along the first centimeter mark. **CAUTION:** *The scalpel is extremely sharp. Handle it carefully.* After cutting the foil, gently place the ruler through the slit until it makes contact with the clay in the box. Be sure to hold the ruler straight. Take the depth measurement. Record your data on the graph on the next page.

10. Repeat Step 9 for each point along the foil. When you are done, you should have a depth profile for the entire length of the box along your transect line.

11. Remove the foil from the box and examine the topography of the model.

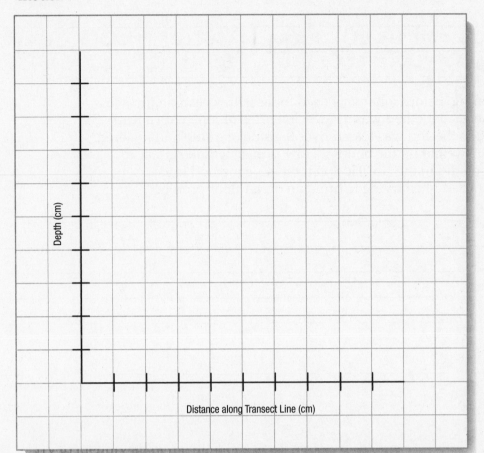

Analyze and Conclude

1. **Inferring** Based on your contour profile, what part of the ocean floor was being modeled? Check your answer with the group that created the model. Were you correct? Why or why not?

_____

_____

_____

_____

2. **Comparing** How does the profile on the graph compare with the contour of the model? Are there any major features in the model that did not appear on your graph? Why or why not?

_____

_____

_____

_____

_____

Name _____ Class _____ Date _____

3. **Analyzing Data** What could you have done to make your profile match the topography more accurately?

_____

_____

_____

4. **Explaining** Before sonar was used to measure ocean depth, a less sophisticated method was used. A long line of rope with a lead weight on the end was tossed over the side of a ship and lowered until the weight hit the bottom. How is this method similar to what you did in the lab? How can the rope method lead to inaccuracies when trying to build an ocean-floor profile?

_____

_____

_____

_____

_____

_____

_____

Chapter 15 Ocean Water and Ocean Life   **Exploration Lab**

How Does Temperature Affect Water Density?

Ocean water temperatures vary from equator to pole and change with depth. Temperature, like salinity, affects the density of seawater. However, the density of seawater is more sensitive to temperature fluctuations than salinity. Cool surface water, which has a greater density than warm surface water, forms in the polar regions, sinks, and moves toward the tropics.

Problem How can you determine the effects of temperature on water density?

Materials

- 2 100-mL graduated cylinders
- 2 test tubes
- 2 beakers
- food coloring or dye
- stirrer
- ice
- tap water
- graph paper
- colored pencils

Skills Observing, Graphing, Inferring, Drawing Conclusions

Procedure 🖐 🧤 📖 🔧

Part A

1. In a beaker, mix cold tap water with several ice cubes. Stir until the water and ice are well mixed.

2. Fill the graduated cylinder with 100 mL of the cold water from the beaker. The graduated cylinder should not contain any pieces of ice.

3. Put 2 to 3 drops of food coloring or dye in a test tube and fill it half full with hot tap water.

4. Pour the contents of the test tube slowly into the graduated cylinder. Record your observations.

_____

_____

5. Add a test tube full of cold tap water to a beaker. Mix in 2 to 3 drops of food coloring dye and a handful of ice to the beaker. Stir the solution thoroughly.

6. Fill the test tube half full of the solution from Step 5. Do not allow any ice into the test tube.

7. Fill the second graduated cylinder with 100 mL of hot tap water.

8. Pour the test tube of cold liquid slowly into the cylinder of hot water. Record your observations.

_____

_____

9. Clean the glassware and return it along with other materials to your teacher.

Part B

1. Use the graph to plot surface temperature and density.

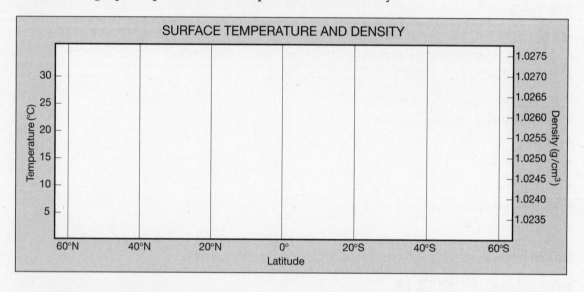

2. Using the information in the Data Table, plot a line on the graph for temperature. Using a different colored pencil, plot a line for density on the same graph.

DATA TABLE Idealized Ocean Surface Water Temperatures and Densities at Various Latitudes

Latitude	Surface Temperature (°C)	Surface Density (g/cm³)
60°N	5	1.0258
40°N	13	1.0259
20°N	24	1.0237
0°	27	1.0238
20°S	24	1.0241
40°S	15	1.0261
60°S	2	1.0272

Analyze and Conclude

1. **Observing** What differences did you observe in the behavior of the two water samples in Part A? Which water sample was the most dense in each experiment?

   _____

   _____

   _____

   _____

2. **Inferring** How does temperature affect the density of water?

   _____

   _____

3. **Drawing Conclusions** If two water samples of equal mass had equal salinities, which sample would be more dense: Water Sample A, which has a temperature of 25°C, or Water Sample B, which has a temperature of 14°C?

   _____

4. **Interpreting Diagrams** Describe the density and temperature characteristics of water in equatorial regions. Compare these characteristics to water found in polar regions.

   _____

   _____

   _____

   _____

5. **Inferring** What is the reason that higher average surface densities are found in the Southern Hemisphere?

   _____

   _____

   _____

6. **Communicating** Write a lab report describing your procedures in this experiment and how you reached your conclusions.

   _____

   _____

   _____

Heating Land and Water

The heating of Earth's surface controls the temperature of the air above it. Different land surfaces absorb varying amounts of incoming solar radiation. The largest contrast, however, is between land and water. The air temperature above water can influence the air temperature over land.

In this lab you will model the difference in the heating of land and water when they are subjected to a source of radiation. You first will assemble simple tools. Then you will observe and record temperature data. Finally, you will explain the results of the experiment and how they relate to the moderating influence of water on air temperatures near Earth's surface.

Problem How do the heating of land and water compare?

Materials

- 2 250-mL beakers
- dry sand
- tap water
- ring stand
- light source
- ruler
- 2 flat wooden sticks
- 2 thermometers
- United States map
- 3 different-colored pencils

Figure 1

Skills Modeling, Observing, Measuring, Analyzing Data

Procedure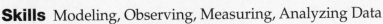

Part A: Preparing for the Experiment

1. Use the Data Table or a computer spreadsheet to record your measurements.

2. Pour 200 mL of dry sand into one of the beakers. Pour 200 mL of water into the other beaker.

3. Hang a light source from a ring stand so that it is about 5 inches above the beaker of sand and the beaker of water. The light should be situated so that it is at the same height above both beakers.

4. Using the wooden sticks, suspend a thermometer in each beaker, as shown in Figure 1. The thermometer bulbs should be just barely below the surfaces of the sand and the water.

5. Record the starting temperatures for both the dry sand and the water in the data table.

Part B: Heating the Beakers

CAUTION: *Do not touch the light source or the beakers without using thermal mitts.*

6. Turn on the light. Observe and record the temperatures in the Data Table at one-minute intervals for 10 minutes.

7. Turn off the light for several minutes. Dampen the sand with water and record the starting temperature for damp sand. Repeat Step 6 for the damp sand.

DATA TABLE Land and Water Heating

	Starting Temperature	1 min	2 min	3 min	4 min	5 min	6 min	7 min	8 min	9 min	10 min
Water											
Dry sand											
Damp sand											

Analyze and Conclude

1. Using Tables and Graphs Use a computer or the graph below to graph the data you collected. Plot the temperatures for the water, dry sand, and damp sand. Use a different-colored line to connect the points for each material.

2. Comparing and Contrasting How does the changing temperature differ for dry sand and water when they are exposed to equal amounts of radiation?

_____

_____

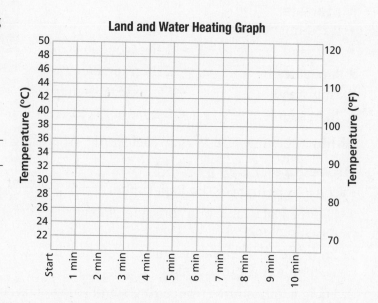

Land and Water Heating Graph

3. Comparing and Contrasting How does the changing temperature differ for dry sand and damp sand when they are exposed to equal amounts of radiation?

_____

4. Applying Locate Eureka, California, and Lafayette, Indiana, on a United States map. Infer which city would show the greater annual temperature range. Explain your answer.

_____

_____

5. Communicating Write a lab report explaining your procedures and conclusions for this lab.

Chapter 18 Moisture, Clouds, and Precipitation

Measuring Humidity

Relative humidity is a measurement used to describe water vapor in the air. In general, it expresses how close the air is to saturation. In this lab, you will use a psychrometer and a data table to determine the relative humidity of air.

Problem How can relative humidity be determined?

Materials
- calculator
- water at room temperature
- psychrometer

Alternative materials for psychrometer:
- 2 thermometers
- cotton gauze
- paper fan
- string

Skills Observing, Measuring, Analyzing Data, Calculating

Procedure 🔧 ✂️
Part A: Calculating Relative Humidity from Water Vapor Content

1. Use Data Table 1 to record your measurements.

2. Relative humidity is the ratio of the air's water vapor content to its water vapor capacity at a given temperature. Relative humidity is expressed as a percent.

$$\text{Relative humidity (\%)} = \frac{\text{Water vapor content}}{\text{Water vapor capacity}} \times 100\%$$

3. At 25°C, the water vapor capacity is 20 g/kg. Use this information to complete Data Table 1.

DATA TABLE 1 Relative Humidity Determination Based on Water Vapor Content

Air temperature (°C)	Water Vapor Content (g/kg)	Water Vapor Capacity (g/kg)	Relative Humidity (%)
25	5	20	25
25	12		
25	18		

Name _____ Class _____ Date _____

Part B: Determining Relative Humidity Using a Psychrometer

4. A psychrometer consists of two thermometers—a wet-bulb thermometer and a dry-bulb thermometer. The wet-bulb thermometer has a cloth wick that is wet with water and spun for about 1 minute. Relative humidity is determined by calculating the difference in the temperature reading between the dry-bulb temperature and the wet-bulb temperature and using Data Table 2. For example, suppose a dry-bulb temperature is measured as 20°C, and a wet-bulb temperature is 14°C. Read the relative humidity from Data Table 2.

_____

5. If a psychrometer is not available, construct a wet-bulb thermometer by tying a piece of cotton gauze around the end of a thermometer. Wet it with room-temperature water, and fan it until the temperature stops changing.

6. Make wet-bulb and dry-bulb temperature measurements for the air in your classroom and the air outside. Use Data Table 3 to record your measurements. Use your measurements and Data Table 2 to determine the relative humidity inside and outside.

DATA TABLE 2 Relative Humidity (percent)

Dry-Bulb Tempera-ture (°C)	Depression of Wet-Bulb Temperature (Dry-Bulb Temperature − Wet-Bulb Temperature = Depression of the Wet Bulb)																					
	1	2	3	4	5	6	7	8	9	10	11	12	13	14	15	16	17	18	19	20	21	22
−20	28																					
−18	40																					
−16	48	0																				
−14	55	11																				
−12	61	23																				
−10	66	33	0																			
−8	71	41	13																			
−6	73	48	20	0																		
−4	77	54	43	11																		
−2	79	58	37	20	1																	
0	81	63	45	28	11																	
2	83	67	51	36	20	6																
4	85	70	56	42	27	14																
6	86	72	59	46	35	22	10	0														
8	87	74	62	51	39	28	17	6														
10	88	76	65	54	43	33	24	13	4													
12	88	78	67	57	48	38	28	19	10	2												
14	89	79	69	60	50	41	33	25	16	8	1											
16	90	80	71	62	54	45	37	29	21	14	7	1										
18	91	81	72	64	56	48	40	33	26	19	12	6	0									
20	91	82	74	66	58	51	44	36	30	23	17	11	5	0								
22	92	83	75	68	60	53	46	40	33	27	21	15	10	4	0							
24	92	84	76	69	62	55	49	42	36	30	25	20	14	9	4	0						
26	92	85	77	70	64	57	51	45	39	34	28	23	18	13	9	5						
28	93	86	78	71	65	59	53	47	42	36	31	26	21	17	12	8	2					
30	93	86	79	72	66	61	55	49	44	39	34	29	25	20	16	12	8	4				
32	93	86	80	73	68	62	56	51	46	41	36	32	27	22	19	14	11	8	4			
34	93	86	81	74	69	63	58	52	48	43	38	34	30	26	22	18	14	11	8	5		
36	94	87	81	75	69	64	59	54	50	44	40	36	32	28	24	21	17	13	10	7	4	
38	94	87	82	76	70	66	60	55	51	46	42	38	34	30	26	23	20	16	13	10	7	5
40	94	89	82	76	71	67	61	57	52	48	44	40	36	33	29	25	22	19	16	13	10	7

Relative Humidity Values

Name _____ Class _____ Date _____

DATA TABLE 3 Relative Humidity Determinations Using Dry- and Wet-Bulb Thermometers

	Inside	Outside
Dry-bulb temperature (°C)		
Wet-bulb temperature (°C)		
Differences between dry-bulb and wet-bulb temperatures (°C)		
Relative humidity (%)		

Analyze and Conclude

1. **Comparing and Contrasting** How do the relative humidity measurements for inside and outside compare? Why are your determinations similar or different?

_____

_____

_____

_____

2. **Applying Concepts** Explain the principle behind using a psychrometer to determine relative humidity.

_____

_____

_____

_____

3. **Applying Concepts** Suppose you hear on the radio that the relative humidity is 90 percent on a winter day. Can you conclude that this air contains more moisture than air on a summer day with a 40 percent relative humidity? Explain why or why not.

_____

_____

_____

_____

4. **Applying Concepts** Why is a cool basement often damp in the summer?

_____

_____

_____

Name _____ Class _____ Date _____

Chapter 19   Air Pressure and Wind

Observing Wind Patterns

Atmospheric pressure and wind are two elements of weather that are closely interrelated. Most people don't usually pay close attention to the pressure given in a weather report. However, pressure differences in the atmosphere drive the winds that often bring changes in temperature and moisture.

Problem How can surface barometric pressure maps be interpreted?

Materials
- Resource 21 in the DataBank

Northern Hemisphere

HIGH   LOW

Skills Observing, Analyzing Data, Calculating

Procedure

1. Look at Figure 2 on the next page. This map shows surface global wind patterns and average global barometric pressure for the month of January.

2. Examine the individual pressure cells—the isobars around the letters H and L—in Figure 2. Then complete the diagrams in your copy of Figure 1. Label the isobars with appropriate pressures, and use arrows to indicate the surface air movement in each pressure cell.

3. Indicate the movements of air in high and low pressure cells by completing the Data Table below.

Southern Hemisphere

HIGH   LOW

Figure 1

DATA TABLE Air Movements in Pressure Cells

Air Movement	N. Hem. High	N. Hem. Low	S. Hem. High	S. Hem. Low
Into/out of				
Rises/sinks				
Rotates CW/CCW*				

*CW = clockwise; CCW = counterclockwise

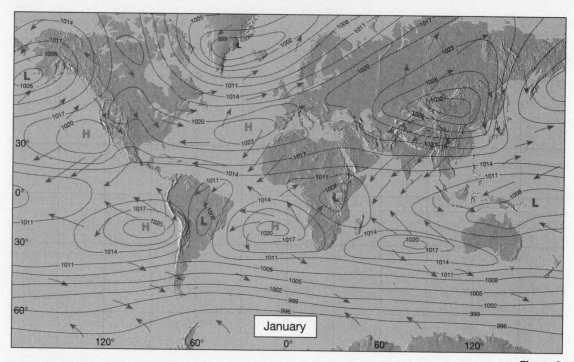

Figure 2

Analyze and Conclude

1. **Comparing and Contrasting** Summarize the differences and
   similarities in surface air movement between a Northern
   Hemisphere cyclone and a Southern Hemisphere cyclone.

   _____

   _____

   _____

   _____

   _____

   _____

   _____

2. **Interpreting Illustrations** Use Resource 21 in the DataBank as a
   reference to locate and write the name of each global wind belt at
   the appropriate location on the map in Figure 2. Also indicate the
   region of the polar front.

3. **Applying** Label the areas on Figure 2 where you would expect
   high wind speeds to occur.

4. **Applying** Label an area on Figure 2 where circulation is most like
   the idealized global wind model for a rotating Earth. Explain why
   this region on Earth is so much like the model.

   _____

   _____

   _____

Middle-Latitude Cyclones

You've learned that much of the day-to-day weather in the United States is caused by middle-latitude cyclones. In this lab, you will identify some of the atmospheric conditions associated with a middle-latitude cyclone. Then you will use what you know about Earth's atmosphere and weather to predict how the movement of the low-pressure system affects weather in the area.

Problem How do middle-latitude cyclones affect weather patterns?

Materials
- colored pencils
- Resource 22 in the DataBank

Skills Observing, Comparing and Contrasting, Predicting

Procedure

1. Use the colored pencils to color the cold air, cool air, and warm air areas on the map in Figure 1. Also color the symbols used to designate the fronts.

2. Identify and label the cold front, warm front, and occluded front on the map in Figure 1.

3. Draw arrows that show the direction of surface winds at points A, C, E, F, and G.

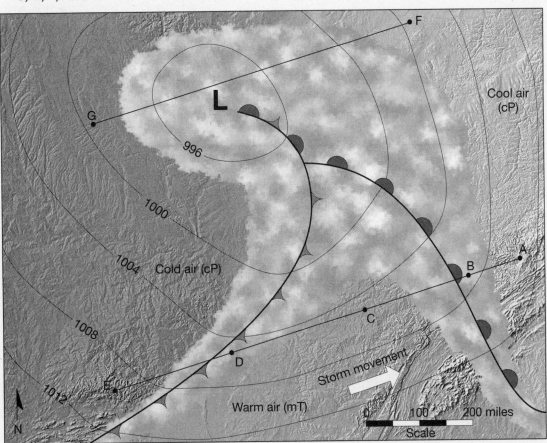

Figure 1

Analyze and Conclude

1. Describing In which direction are the surface winds moving?

_____

_____

_____

_____

2. Identifying At which stage of formation is the cyclone? Explain your answer. Refer to the map on Resource 22 in the DataBank if necessary.

_____

_____

3. Explaining Is the air in the center of the cyclone rising or falling? What effect does this have on the potential for condensation and precipitation?

_____

_____

_____

4. Inferring Find the center of the low, which is marked with the letter *L*. What type of front has formed here? What happens to the maritime tropical air in this type of front?

_____

_____

5. Predicting Once the warm front passes, in which direction will the wind at point B blow?

_____

6. Synthesizing Describe the changes in wind direction and moisture in the air that will likely occur at point D after the cold front passes.

_____

_____

7. Synthesizing Describe the wind directions, humidity, and precipitation expected for a city as the cyclone moves and the city's relative position changes from point A to point B, point C, point D, and finally from point D to point E.

_____

_____

_____

_____

Chapter 21   Climate

Human Impact on Climate and Weather

Scientists are now closely monitoring how daily human activity is changing microclimates. There is concern that changing microclimates can have an effect on global climates. In this investigation, you will explore some of the ways that human activities are changing the atmosphere.

Problem How do we know that human activity is changing Earth's climates?

Materials
- paper
- pen or pencil

Skills Calculating, Measuring, Using Tables, Analyzing Data

Procedure
1. Data Table 1 lists many of the types, sources, and amounts of primary pollutants. Use this table to answer Questions 1, 2, 3, and 4 under Analyze and Conclude.

DATA TABLE 1 Estimated Nationwide Emissions (millions of metric tons/year)

Source	Carbon Monoxide	Partic- ulates	Sulfur Oxides	Volatile Organics	Nitrogen Oxides	Total
Transportation	43.5	1.6	1.0	5.1	7.3	58.5
Stationary source fuel combustion	4.7	1.9	16.6	0.7	10.6	34.5
Industrial processes	4.7	2.6	3.2	7.9	0.6	19.0
Solid waste disposal	2.1	0.3	0.0	0.7	0.1	3.2
Miscellaneous	7.2	1.2	0.0	2.8	0.2	11.4
Total	62.2	7.6	20.8	17.2	18.8	126.6

Source: U.S. Environmental Protection Agency

2. Look at Figure A. The pollutants listed are linked to a wide variety of negative health effects such as eye irritation, heart damage, and lung damage. The pollutants shown are also linked to reduced visibility, reduced crop yields, and damage to ecosystems. Study the figure and answer Questions 5, 6, and 7.

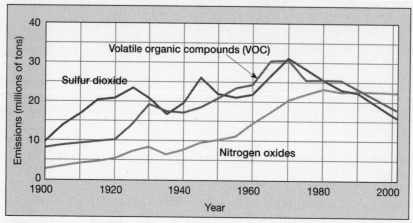

Figure A

3. Look at Figure B. Scientists have noted the increasing levels of carbon dioxide in the atmosphere. Research continues to determine whether these increasing levels are affecting global climates. Use Figure B to answer Question 8.

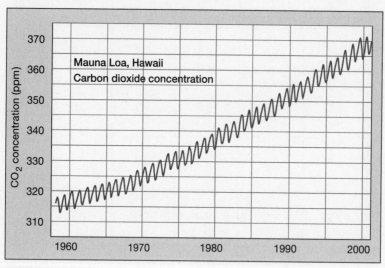

Figure B

4. Look at Data Table 2. This table presents data on the effects of large cities on their surrounding microclimates. Summer temperatures in cities can be higher than the surrounding countryside. Meteorologists call this effect "the urban heat island." Study the data in the table and answer Questions 9, 10, and 11.

Analyze and Conclude

1. **Interpreting Data** What is the leading source (by weight) of primary pollutants? How many metric tons of this pollutant are added to the atmosphere each year?

_____

2. **Interpreting Data** Which of the following is the most abundant primary pollutant?

   a. carbon monoxide

   b. sulfur oxides

_____

3. **Calculating** Your answer for item 2 is what percentage of all primary pollutants?

   a. 25%   **b.** 50%   **c.** 75%

_____

DATA TABLE 2 Average Climatic Changes Produced by Cities

Element	Comparison with Rural Temperature
Particulate matter	10 times more
Temperature	
Annual mean	0.5–1.5°C higher
Winter	1–2°C higher
Solar radiation	15–30% less
Ultraviolet, winter	30% less
Ultraviolet, summer	5% less
Precipitation	5–15% more
Thunderstorm frequency	16% more
Winter	5% more
Summer	29% more
Relative humidity	6% lower
Winter	2% lower
Summer	8% lower
Cloudiness (frequency)	5–10% more
Fog (frequency)	60% more
Winter	100% more
Summer	30% more
Wind speed	25% lower
Calms	5–20% more

Source: After Landsberg, Changnon, and others

4. **Calculating** What is the approximate total weight (in million metric tons) of all primary pollutants added to the atmosphere?

_____

5. **Interpreting Data** Describe the trend you see in the data for atmospheric pollutants prior to 1970.

_____

6. **Interpreting Data** Describe the trend you see in the data for atmospheric pollutants since 1970.

_____

7. **Inferring** Suggest a reason for the changing trends in Questions 5 and 6.

_____

_____

_____

8. **Calculating** What has been the approximate percentage increase in atmospheric carbon dioxide near Mauna Loa since 1958?

_____

_____

9. **Interpreting Data** Compared to rural areas, which factors are increased by urbanization? Which factors are decreased?

_____

_____

10. **Interpreting Data** Of all of the factors shown, which shows the greatest increase due to urbanization?

_____

11. **Predicting** Suggest a possible reason for each of the following effects on the weather that is influenced by a city.

   a. increased frequency of thunderstorms

   b. lower wind speed

   c. increased precipitation

_____

_____

_____

_____

Modeling Synodic and Sidereal Months

The time interval required for the moon to complete a full cycle of phases is 29.5 days, or one synodic month. The true period of the moon's revolution around Earth, however, is only 27.3 days and is known as the sidereal month. In this lab, you will model the differences between synodic and sidereal months.

Problem How do synodic and sidereal months differ?

Materials

- lamp
- basketball
- softball

Skills Observing, Using Models, Analyzing Data, Drawing Conclusions

Procedure

1. On the diagram of Month 1, indicate the dark half of the moon on each of the eight lunar positions by shading the appropriate area with a pencil.

2. On the diagram of Month 1, label the position of the new moon. Do the same for the other lunar phases.

3. Repeat Steps 1 and 2 for the diagram of Month 2.

4. Place the lamp on a desk or table. The lamp represents the sun. Hold the softball, which represents the moon. Have a partner hold the basketball, which represents Earth. Turn on the lamp and turn off all other lights in the room.

5. Stand so that the "moon" is in the position of the new-moon phase in Month 1, relative to "Earth" and the "sun." Revolve the moon around Earth while at the same time moving both Earth and the moon to Month 2. Stop at the same numbered position at which you began. Use the diagrams to guide your movements.

Analyze and Conclude

1. **Using Models** After one complete revolution beginning at the new-moon phase in Month 1, in what position is the moon located in Month 2?

   _____

2. **Interpreting Data** Based on your answer to the previous question, does this position occur before or after the moon has completed one full cycle of phases?

   _____

3. Identifying In Month 2, what position represents the new-moon phase? When the moon reaches this position, will it have completed a synodic or sidereal month?

_____

4. Summarizing In your own words, explain the difference between a sidereal and synodic month.

_____

_____

_____

_____

_____

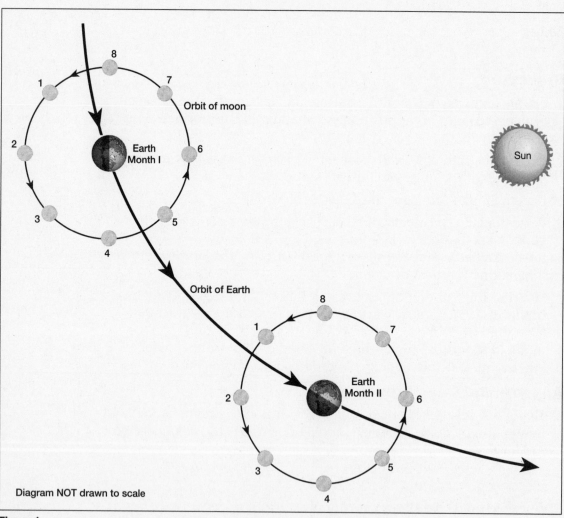

Diagram NOT drawn to scale

Figure 1

Chapter 23   Touring Our Solar System   **Exploration Lab**

Modeling the Solar System

An examination of any scale model of the solar system reveals that the distances from the sun and the spacing between the planets appear to follow a regular pattern. The best way to examine this pattern is to build an actual scale model of the solar system.

Problem How can you model distances among the planets and their distances from the sun?

Materials

- meter stick
- calculator
- colored pencils
- 6-meter length of adding machine paper

Skills Calculating, Using Models

Procedure

Note: Use Figure 1 on the next page to help you model the solar system.

1. Place the 6-meter length of adding machine paper on the floor.

2. Draw an X about 10 centimeters from one end of the adding machine paper. Label this mark "sun."

3. The Data Table shows the mean distances of the planets and Pluto from the sun, as well as their diameters. Use the table and the following scale to calculate the proper scale distance of each object from the sun:

   1 millimeter = 1 million kilometers

   1 centimeter = 10 million kilometers

   1 meter = 1000 million kilometers

4. After calculating the scale distances, draw on a separate sheet of paper a small circle for each object at its proper scale distance from the sun. Use a different-colored pencil for the inner and outer planets and for Pluto. Write the name of each object next to its position.

DATA TABLE

Planet	Distance from Sun		Diameter (km)	Scale Distance from Sun
	AU	Millions of km		
Mercury	0.39	58	4878	
Venus	0.72	108	12,104	
Earth	1.00	150	12,756	
Mars	1.52	228	6794	
Jupiter	5.20	778	143,884	
Saturn	9.54	1427	120,536	
Uranus	19.18	2870	51,118	
Neptune	30.06	4497	50,530	
Pluto*	39.44	5900	2300	

*Note that Pluto is a dwarf planet.

Name _____ Class _____ Date _____

Analyze and Conclude

1. Using Models How far from the sun is Earth located on your model? How far from the sun are the rest of the planets located? Where is Pluto located?

_____

_____

_____

2. Observing What pattern of spacing do you observe? Summarize the pattern for both the inner and outer planets.

_____

_____

_____

_____

3. Interpreting Data Which object or objects vary most from the general pattern of spacing?

_____

_____

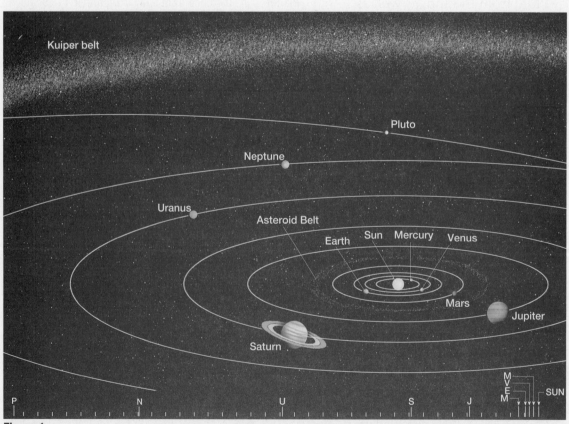

Figure 1

Chapter 24   Studying the Sun   **Exploration Lab**

Tracking Sunspots

Sunspots begin as small areas about 1600 kilometers in diameter. Most last for only a few hours. However, some grow into dark regions many times larger than Earth and last for a month or more. In this lab you will count the number of sunspots over the course of several days.

Problem How can you use a telescope to safely view and count the number of sunspots on the sun's surface?

Materials
- telescope
- large cardboard box
- metric ruler
- small cardboard box
- piece of white paper
- tape

Skills Observing, Interpreting Data, Making and Using Graphs

Procedure ✂ ⚠

⚠ 1. Position a telescope on a tripod outside in a sunny spot away from trees and other obstacles. The eyepiece should face away from the sun. **CAUTION:** *Never look at the sun directly. Do not view the sun through the telescope. These actions could cause eye damage.*

2. Place the large cardboard box on the ground about 15 centimeters in front of the telescope's eyepiece.

3. Use the pencil to punch a hole in one side of the small cardboard box. Tape a sheet of white paper inside the opposite end of the box, as shown in the illustration.

4. Place the small box on top of the large box so that its front is open for viewing. The hole in the small box should face the eyepiece of the telescope. Adjust the telescope so that the eyepiece, the hole, and the white paper are aligned.

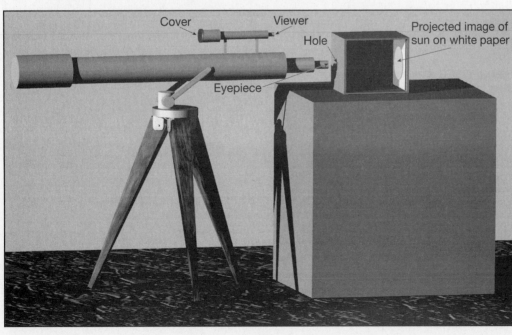

Cover   Viewer   Hole   Projected image of sun on white paper   Eyepiece

Name _____ Class _____ Date _____

5. Adjust the small box until you see an image of the sun projected onto the paper. You may adjust the telescope to obtain a clearer image, but do not look through the viewer to accomplish this. You may also vary the distance between the box and the telescope to obtain better images.

6. Record the number of sunspots that you observe in the Data Table. Trace the outlines of sunspots on the paper in the box. Shade in the sunspots and use the ruler to measure their size.

7. As weather permits, make several more viewings of sunspots over the course of the next few days. During each viewing, repeat Steps 1–6. Be sure to note the movement of the sunspots in the Data Table.

DATA TABLE

Day	Number of Sunspots	Movement?
1		
2		
3		
4		
5		

Analyze and Conclude

1. **Making Graphs** How many sunspots did you observe? Make a line graph of the data from your data table.

_____

_____

2. **Observing** How did the number of sunspots vary over the course of your observations?

_____

_____

_____

_____

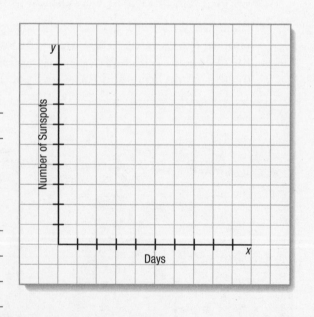

3. **Interpreting Data** Why did the sunspots move?

_____

_____

Observing Stars

Throughout history, people have been recording the nightly movement of stars that results from Earth's rotation, as well as the seasonal changes in the constellations as Earth revolves around the sun. Early astronomers offered many explanations for the changes before the true nature of the motions was understood in the seventeenth century. In this lab, you'll observe and identify stars.

Problem How can you use star charts to identify constellations and track star movements?

Materials
- Resource 19 in the DataBank
- Resource 21 in the DataBank
- penlight
- notebook

Skills Observing, Summarizing, Interpreting Data

Procedure
1. On a clear, moonless night go outside and stand as far from street lights as possible. Observe the stars.

2. In the Data Table, record the date and make a list of the different colors of stars that you see.

3. Select one star that is overhead or nearly so. Observe and record its movement over a period of one hour. Also note the direction of its movement (eastward, westward).

DATA TABLE

Date	Star Colors	Star Movement	Constellations	Motions of Stars Around North Star

4. Select a star chart suitable for your location and season. Locate and record the names of several constellations that you see in the sky. Sketch and label them in the box below.

5. Locate the North Star (Polaris) in the night sky. Observe and record the motion of stars that surround the North Star.

6. Repeat your observations several weeks later at the same location.

Name _____ Class _____ Date _____

Analyze and Conclude

1. **Observing** How many different colors of stars did you observe? How do these colors relate to star temperature? *Hint:* The Hertzsprung-Russell diagram in the Appendix may help you.

_____

_____

_____

_____

2. **Interpreting Data** In which direction did the star that you observed appear to move? How is this movement related to the direction of Earth's rotation?

_____

_____

_____

_____

3. **Summarizing** Write a brief summary of the motion of the stars that surround the North Star. Be sure to include any changes you observed during your second viewing.

_____

_____

_____

_____

Control data and monuments
Vertical control

Third order or better, with tablet	BM ×16.3
Third order or better, recoverable mark	× 120.0
Bench mark at found section corner	BM 18.6
Spot elevation	× 5.3

Contours
Topographic

Intermediate	
Index	
Supplementary	
Depression	
Cut; fill	

Bathymetric

Intermediate	
Index	
Primary	
Index primary	
Supplementary	

Boundaries

National	
State or territorial	
County or equivalent	
Civil township or equivalent	
Incorporated city or equivalent	
Park, reservation, or monument	

Surface features

Levee	Levee
Sand or mud area, dunes, or shifting sand	Sand
Intricate surface area	Strip mine
Gravel beach or glacial moraine	Gravel
Tailings pond	Tailings pond

Mines and caves

Quarry or open pit mine	
Gravel, sand, clay, or borrow pit	
Mine dump	Mine dump
Tailings	Tailings

Vegetation

Woods	
Scrub	
Orchard	
Vineyard	
Mangrove	Mangrove

Glaciers and permanent snowfields

Contours and limits	
Form lines	

Marine shoreline
Topographic maps

Approximate mean high water	
Indefinite or unsurveyed	

Topographic-bathymetric maps

Mean high water	
Apparent (edge of vegetation)	

Coastal features

Foreshore flat	
Rock or coral reef	
Rock bare or awash	
Group of rocks bare or awash	
Exposed wreck	
Depth curve; sounding	
Breakwater, pier, jetty, or wharf	
Seawall	

Rivers, lakes, and canals

Intermittent stream	
Intermittent river	
Disappearing stream	
Perennial stream	
Perennial river	
Small falls; small rapids	
Large falls; large rapids	
Masonry dam	
Dam with lock	
Dam carrying road	
Perennial lake; Intermittent lake or pond	
Dry lake	Dry lake
Narrow wash	
Wide wash	Wide wash
Canal, flume, or aquaduct with lock	
Well or spring; spring or seep	

Submerged areas and bogs

Marsh or swamp	
Submerged marsh or swamp	
Wooded marsh or swamp	
Submerged wooded marsh or swamp	
Rice field	Rice
Land subject to inundation	Max pool 431

Buildings and related features

Building	
School; church	
Built-up area	
Racetrack	
Airport	
Landing strip	
Well (other than water); windmill	
Tanks	
Covered reservoir	
Gaging station	
Landmark object (feature as labeled)	
Campground; picnic area	
Cemetery: small; large	Cem

Roads and related features

Roads on Provisional edition maps are not classified as primary, secondary, or light duty. They are all symbolized as light duty roads.

Primary highway	
Secondary highway	
Light duty road	
Unimproved road	
Trail	
Dual highway	
Dual highway with median strip	

Railroads and related features

Standard gauge single track; station	
Standard gauge multiple track	
Abandoned	

Transmission lines and pipelines

Power transmission line; pole; tower	
Telephone line	Telephone
Aboveground oil or gas pipeline	
Underground oil or gas pipeline	Pipeline

Symbols used on topographic quadrangle maps produced by the U.S. Geological Survey. Variations will be found on older maps.

DataBank

Crystal A

Crystal B

Crystal D

Crystal C

Crystal E

Crystal F

Crystal G

Crystal H

Crystal J

Crystal I

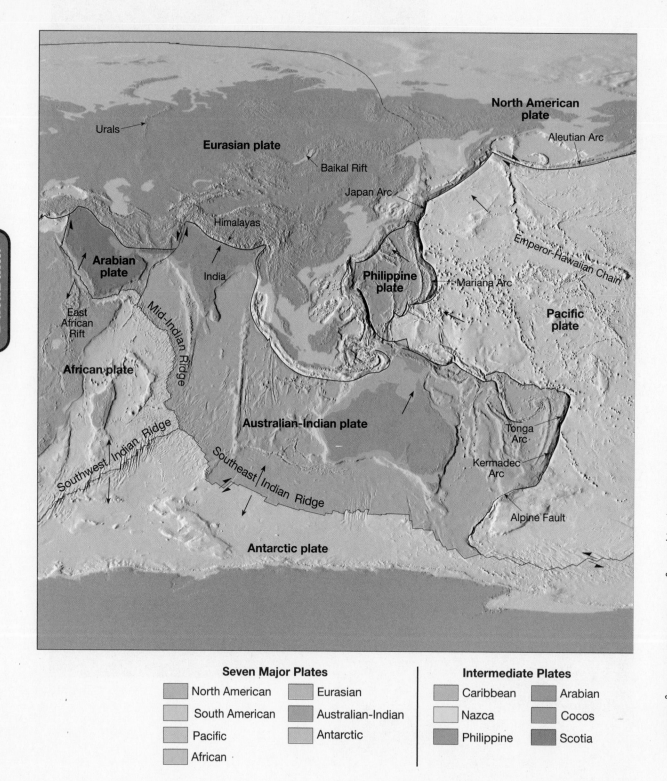

Seven Major Plates

- North American
- South American
- Pacific
- African
- Eurasian
- Australian-Indian
- Antarctic

Intermediate Plates

- Caribbean
- Nazca
- Philippine
- Arabian
- Cocos
- Scotia

North American
plate

Canadian Shield

Iceland

Eurasian plate

Rocky Mountains

Basin
and
Range

Appalachian Mts.

Alps

Juan de Fuca
plate

San Andreas
Fault

Caribbean
plate

African plate

Cocos
plate

Antilles
Arc

Mid-Atlantic Ridge

Pacific plate

Galapagos
Ridge

South American
plate

East Pacific Rise

Andes Mountains

Nazca
plate

Chile Ridge

Scotia plate

Antarctic plate

DataBank

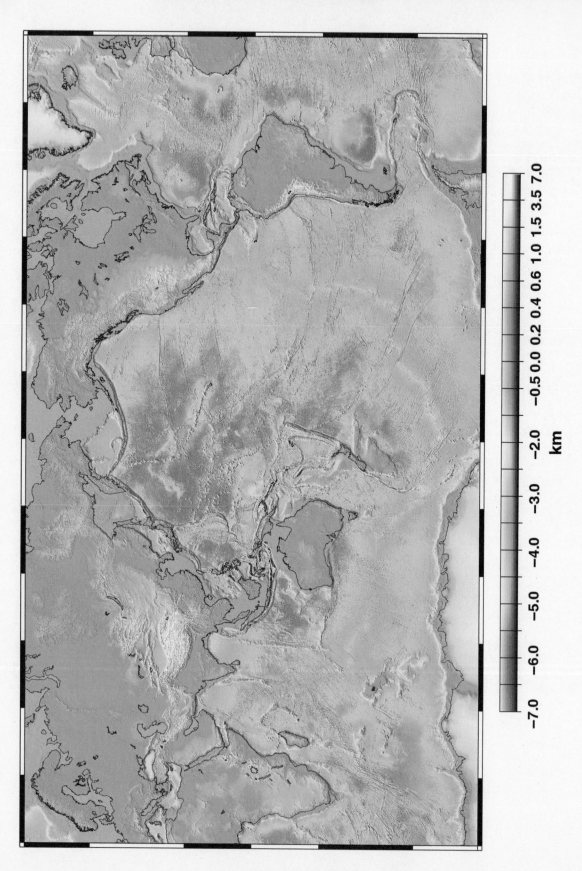

-7.0 -6.0 -5.0 -4.0 -3.0 -2.0 -0.5 0.0 0.2 0.4 0.6 1.0 1.5 3.5 7.0

km

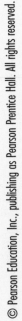

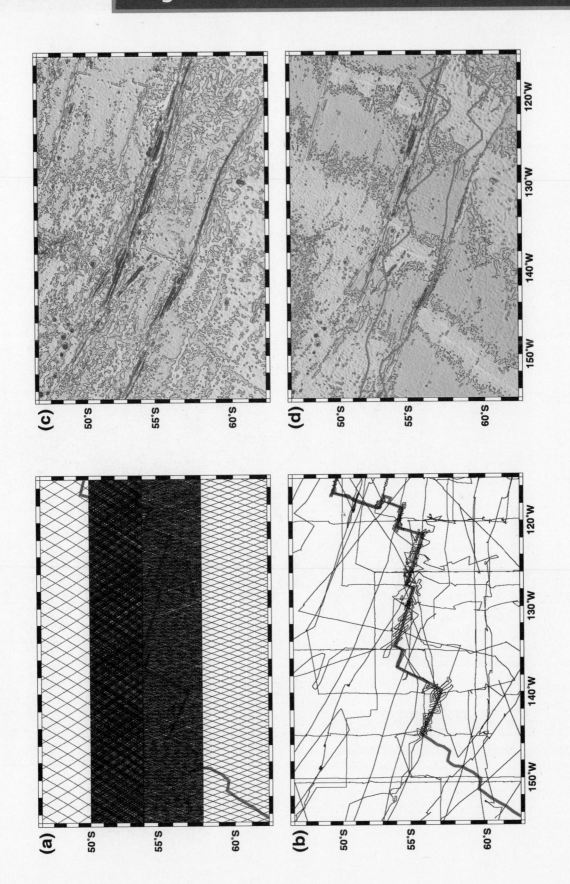

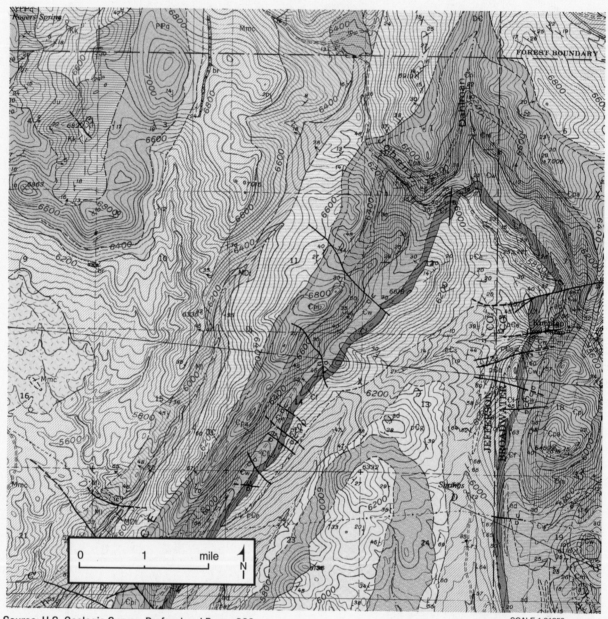

Source: U.S. Geologic Survey, Professional Paper 292

SCALE 1:31250
CONTOUR INTERVAL 40 FEET
DATUM IS MEAN SEA LEVEL

DataBank

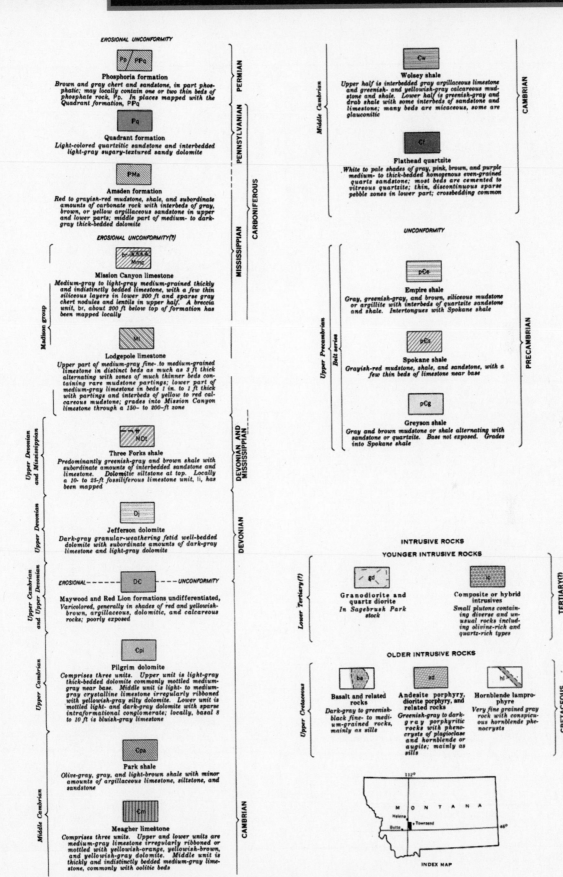

EROSIONAL UNCONFORMITY

Pp / PPq

Phosphoria formation
Brown and gray chert and sandstone, in part phosphatic; may locally contain one or two thin beds of phosphate rock, Pp. In places mapped with the Quadrant formation, PPq

PERMIAN

Pq

Quadrant formation
Light-colored quartzitic sandstone and interbedded light-gray sugary-textured sandy dolomite

PENNSYLVANIAN

PMa

Amsden formation
Red to grayish-red mudstone, shale, and subordinate amounts of carbonate rock with interbeds of gray, brown, or yellow argillaceous sandstone in upper and lower parts; middle part of medium- to dark-gray thick-bedded dolomite

EROSIONAL UNCONFORMITY(?)

CARBONIFEROUS

br · Mmc

Mission Canyon limestone
Medium-gray to light-gray medium-grained thickly and indistinctly bedded limestone, with a few thin siliceous layers in lower 200 ft and sparse gray chert nodules and lentils in upper half. A breccia unit, br, about 200 ft below top of formation has been mapped locally

MISSISSIPPIAN

Madison group

Ml

Lodgepole limestone
Upper part of medium-gray fine- to medium-grained limestone in distinct beds as much as 3 ft thick alternating with zones of much thinner beds containing rare mudstone partings; lower part of medium-gray limestone in beds 1 in. to 1 ft thick with partings and interbeds of yellow to red calcareous mudstone; grades into Mission Canyon limestone through a 150- to 200-ft zone

DEVONIAN AND MISSISSIPPIAN

Upper Devonian and Mississippian

MDt

Three Forks shale
Predominantly greenish-gray and brown shale with subordinate amounts of interbedded sandstone and limestone. Dolomitic siltstone at top. Locally a 10- to 25-ft fossiliferous limestone unit, li, has been mapped

Upper Devonian

Dj

Jefferson dolomite
Dark-gray granular-weathering fetid well-bedded dolomite with subordinate amounts of dark-gray limestone and light-gray dolomite

DEVONIAN

EROSIONAL — — — — — UNCONFORMITY

DC

Maywood and Red Lion formations undifferentiated,
Varicolored, generally in shades of red and yellowish-brown, argillaceous, dolomitic, and calcareous rocks; poorly exposed

Upper Cambrian and Upper Devonian

Cpi

Pilgrim dolomite
Comprises three units. Upper unit is light-gray thick-bedded dolomite commonly mottled medium-gray near base. Middle unit is light- to medium-gray crystalline limestone irregularly ribboned with yellowish-gray silty dolomite. Lower unit is mottled light- and dark-gray dolomite with sparse intraformational conglomerate; locally, basal 8 to 10 ft is bluish-gray limestone

Upper Cambrian

Cpa

Park shale
Olive-gray, gray, and light-brown shale with minor amounts of argillaceous limestone, siltstone, and sandstone

CAMBRIAN

Cm

Meagher limestone
Comprises three units. Upper and lower units are medium-gray limestone irregularly ribboned or mottled with yellowish-orange, yellowish-brown, and yellowish-gray dolomite. Middle unit is thickly and indistinctly bedded medium-gray limestone, commonly with oolitic beds

Middle Cambrian

Cw

Wolsey shale
Upper half is interbedded gray argillaceous limestone and greenish- and yellowish-gray calcareous mudstone and shale. Lower half is greenish-gray and drab shale with some interbeds of sandstone and limestone; many beds are micaceous, some are glauconitic

Middle Cambrian

Cf

Flathead quartzite
White to pale shades of gray, pink, brown, and purple medium- to thick-bedded homogenous even-grained quartz sandstone; most beds are cemented to vitreous quartzite; thin, discontinuous sparse pebble zones in lower part; crossbedding common

CAMBRIAN

UNCONFORMITY

pCe

Empire shale
Gray, greenish-gray, and brown, siliceous mudstone or argillite with interbeds of quartzite sandstone and shale. Intertongues with Spokane shale

Belt series

Upper Precambrian

pCs

Spokane shale
Grayish-red mudstone, shale, and sandstone, with a few thin beds of limestone near base

pCg

Greyson shale
Gray and brown mudstone or shale alternating with sandstone or quartzite. Base not exposed. Grades into Spokane shale

PRECAMBRIAN

INTRUSIVE ROCKS

YOUNGER INTRUSIVE ROCKS

Lower Tertiary(?)

gd

Granodiorite and quartz diorite
In Sagebrush Park stock

ic

Composite or hybrid intrusives
Small plutons containing diverse and unusual rocks including olivine-rich and quartz-rich types

TERTIARY(?)

OLDER INTRUSIVE ROCKS

Upper Cretaceous

ba

Basalt and related rocks
Dark-gray to greenish-black fine- to medium-grained rocks, mainly as sills

ad

Andesite porphyry, diorite porphyry, and related rocks
Greenish-gray to dark-gray porphyritic rocks with phenocrysts of plagioclase and hornblende or augite; mainly as sills

hl

Hornblende lamprophyre
Very fine grained gray rock with conspicuous hornblende phenocrysts

CRETACEOUS

112°

M O N T A N A

Helena

Butte Townsend

46°

INDEX MAP

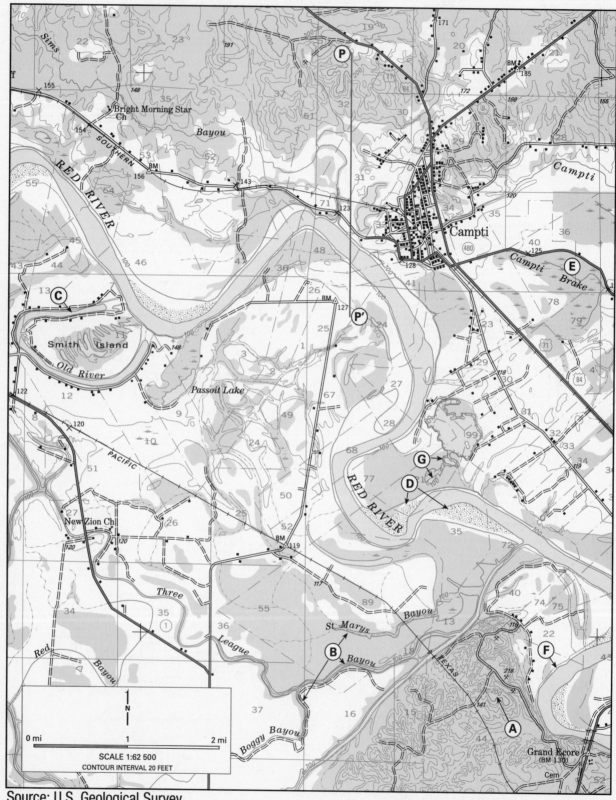

DataBank

SCALE 1:62 500
CONTOUR INTERVAL 20 FEET

0 mi   1   2 mi

Source: U.S. Geological Survey

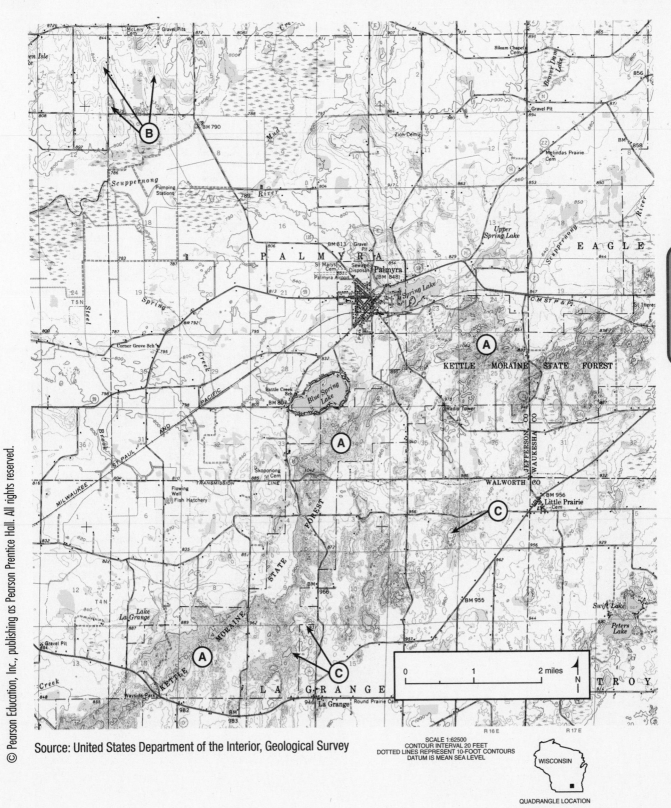

DataBank

Source: United States Department of the Interior, Geological Survey

SCALE 1:62500
CONTOUR INTERVAL 20 FEET
DOTTED LINES REPRESENT 10-FOOT CONTOURS
DATUM IS MEAN SEA LEVEL

WISCONSIN

QUADRANGLE LOCATION

Eon	Era	Millions of Years Ago
Phanerozoic	Cenozoic	65
	Mesozoic	248
	Paleozoic	540
Precambrian	Proterozoic — Late	900
	Proterozoic — Middle	1600
	Proterozoic — Early	2500
	Archean — Late	3000
	Archean — Middle	3400
	Archean — Early	3800
	Hadean	
	Origin of Earth	4500

Era	Period	Epoch	Millions of Years Ago	Development of Plants and Animals
Cenozoic	Quaternary	Holocene	0.01	Humans develop
		Pleistocene	1.8	
	Tertiary	Pliocene	5.3	"Age of Mammals"
		Miocene	23.8	
		Oligocene	33.7	
		Eocene	54.8	
		Paleocene	65.0	Extinction of dinosaurs and many other species
Mesozoic	Cretaceous			First flowering plants
			144	
	Jurassic			First birds
			206	
	Triassic			Dinosaurs dominant
			248	
Paleozoic	Permian			Extinction of trilobites and many other marine animals
			290	
	Carboniferous — Pennsylvanian			First reptiles
			323	Large coal swamps
	Carboniferous — Mississippian			Amphibians abundant
			354	
	Devonian			First insect fossils
				Fishes dominant
	Silurian		417	First land plants
			443	
	Ordovician			First fishes
			490	
	Cambrian			Trilobites dominant
				First organisms with shells
			540	
Precambrian				First multicelled organisms

CENOZOIC ERA (Age of Recent Life)	**Quaternary Period**	*Pecten gibbus*		*Neptunea tabulata*	
	Tertiary Period	*Calyptraphorus velatus*		*Venericardia planicosta*	
MESOZOIC ERA (Age of Medieval Life)	**Cretaceous Period**	*Scaphites hippocrepis*		*Inoceramus labiatus*	
	Jurassic Period	*Perisphinctes tiziani*		*Nerinea trinodosa*	
	Triassic Period	*Trophites subbullatus*		*Monotis subcircularis*	
PALEOZOIC ERA (Age of Ancient Life)	**Permian Period**	*Leptodus americanus*		*Parafusulina bosei*	
	Pennsylvanian Period	*Dictyoclostus americanus*		*Lophophyllidium proliferum*	
	Mississippian Period	*Cactocrinus multibrachiatus*		*Prolecanites gurleyi*	
	Devonian Period	*Mucrospirifer mucronatus*		*Palmatolepus unicornis*	
	Silurian Period	*Cystiphyllum niagarense*		*Hexamoceras hertzeri*	
	Ordovician Period	*Bathyurus extans*		*Tetragraptus fructicosus*	
	Cambrian Period	*Paradoxides pinus*		*Billingsella corrugata*	
PRECAMBRIAN	– – – –				

DataBank

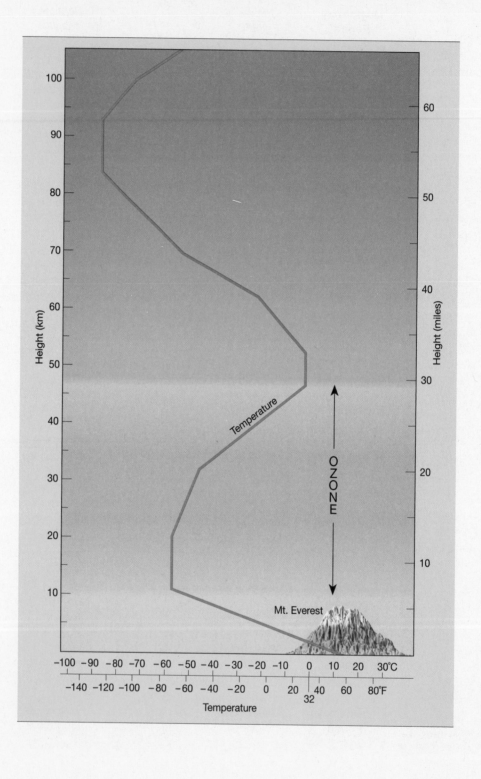

DataBank

Dew-Point Temperature (°C)

(Dry-Bulb Temperature Minus Wet-Bulb Temperature = Depression of the Wet Bulb)

Dry-Bulb (Air) Temperature — *Dew-Point Values*

Dry Bulb (°C)	1	2	3	4	5	6	7	8	9	10	11	12	13	14	15	16	17	18	19	20	21	22
-20	-33																					
-18	-28																					
-16	-24																					
-14	-21	-36																				
-12	-18	-28																				
-10	-14	-22																				
-8	-12	-18	-29																			
-6	-10	-14	-22																			
-4	-7	-12	-17	-29																		
-2	-5	-8	-13	-20																		
0	-3	-6	-9	-15	-24																	
2	-1	-3	-6	-11	-17																	
4	1	-1	-4	-7	-11	-19																
6	4	1	-1	-4	-7	-13	-21															
8	6	3	1	-2	-5	-9	-14															
10	8	6	4	1	-2	-5	-9	-14	-18													
12	10	8	6	4	1	-2	-5	-9	-16													
14	12	10	9	6	4	1	-2	-5	-10	-17												
16	14	12	11	9	7	4	1	-1	-6	-10	-17											
18	16	15	13	11	9	7	4	2	-2	-5	-10	-19										
20	19	17	15	14	12	10	7	4	2	-2	-5	-10	-19									
22	21	19	17	16	14	12	10	8	5	3	-1	-5	-10	-19								
24	23	21	20	18	16	14	12	10	8	6	2	-1	-5	-10	-18							
26	25	23	22	20	18	17	15	13	11	9	6	3	0	-4	-9	-18						
28	27	25	24	22	21	19	17	16	14	11	9	7	4	1	-3	-9	-16					
30	29	27	26	24	23	21	19	18	16	14	12	10	8	5	1	-2	-8	-15				
32	31	29	28	27	25	24	22	20	19	17	15	13	11	8	5	2	-2	-7	-14			
34	33	31	30	29	27	26	24	23	21	20	18	16	14	12	9	6	3	-1	-5	-12	-29	
36	35	33	32	31	29	28	27	25	24	22	20	19	17	15	13	10	7	4	0	-4	-10	
38	37	35	34	33	32	30	29	28	26	25	23	21	19	17	15	13	11	8	5	1	-3	-9
40	39	37	36	35	34	32	31	30	28	27	25	24	22	20	18	16	14	12	9	6	2	-2

DataBank

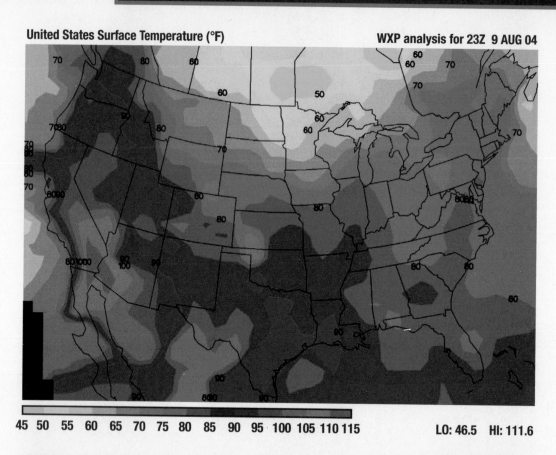

United States Surface Temperature (°F)

WXP analysis for 23Z 9 AUG 04

45 50 55 60 65 70 75 80 85 90 95 100 105 110 115

LO: 46.5 HI: 111.6

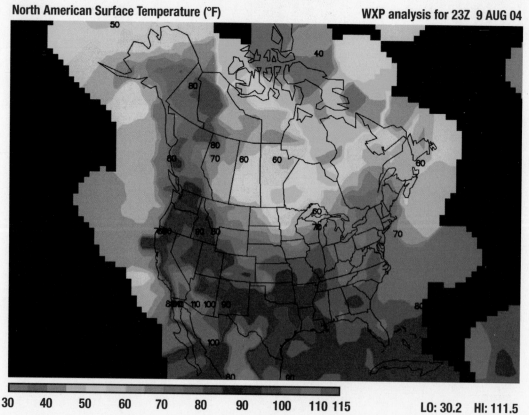

North American Surface Temperature (°F)

WXP analysis for 23Z 9 AUG 04

30 40 50 60 70 80 90 100 110 115

LO: 30.2 HI: 111.5

DataBank

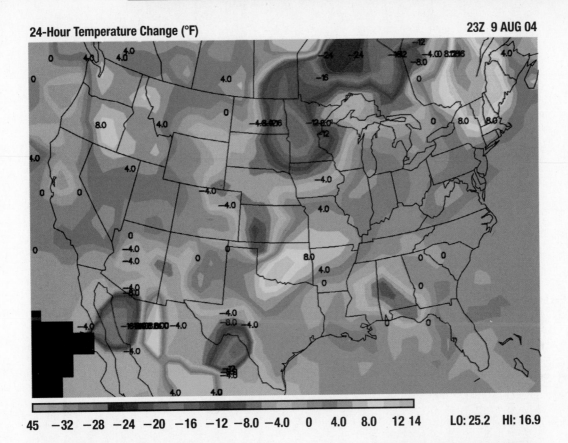

24-Hour Temperature Change (°F)   23Z 9 AUG 04

45   −32   −28   −24   −20   −16   −12   −8.0   −4.0   0   4.0   8.0   12 14   LO: 25.2   HI: 16.9

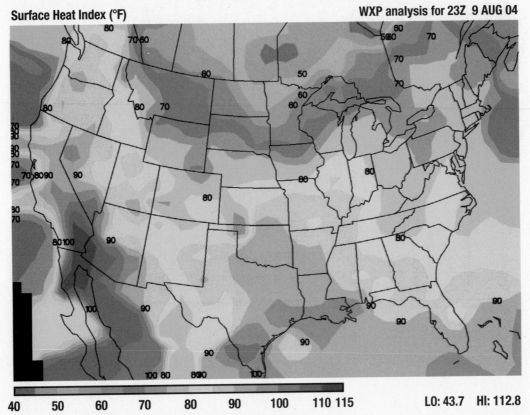

Surface Heat Index (°F)   WXP analysis for 23Z 9 AUG 04

40   50   60   70   80   90   100   110 115   LO: 43.7   HI: 112.8

DataBank

Name	Chemical Formula and Mineral Group	Common Color(s)	Density (g/cm³)	Hardness	Comments
Quartz	SiO_2 silicates	colorless, milky white, pink, brown	2.65	7	glassy luster; conchoidal fractures
Orthoclase feldspar	$KAlSi_3O_8$ silicates	white to pink	2.57	6	cleaves in two directions at 90°
Plagioclase feldspar	$(Na,Ca)AlSi_3O_8$ silicates	white to gray	2.69*	6	cleaves in two directions at 90°; striations common
Galena	PbS sulfides	metallic silver	7.5*	2.5	cleaves in two directions at 90°; lead gray streak
Pyrite	FeS_2 sulfides	brassy yellow	5.02	6–6.5	fractures; forms cubic crystals; greenish-black streak
Sulfur	S native elements	yellow	2.07*	1.5–2.5	fractures; yellow streak smells like rotten eggs
Fluorite	CaF_2 halides	colorless, purple	3.18	4	perfect cleavage in four directions; glassy luster
Olivine	$(Mg,Fe)_2SiO_4$ silicates	green, yellowish-green	3.82*	6.5–7	fractures; glassy luster; often has granular texture
Calcite	$CaCO_3$ carbonates	colorless, gray	2.71	3	bubbles with HCl; cleaves in three directions
Talc	$Mg_3Si_4O_{10}(OH)_2$ silicates	pale green, gray, white	2.75*	1	pearly luster; feels greasy; cleaves in one direction
Gypsum	$CaSO_4 \cdot 2H_2O$ sulfates	colorless, white, gray	2.32	2	glassy or pearly luster; cleaves in three directions
Muscovite mica	$KAl_3Si_3O_{10}(OH)_2$ silicates	colorless in thin sheets to brown	2.82*	2–2.5	silky to pearly luster; cleaves in one direction to form flexible sheets

* Average density of the mineral

Name	Chemical Formula and Mineral Group	Common Color(s)	Density (g/cm³)	Hardness	Comments
Biotite mica	$K(Mg,Fe)_3(AlSi_3O_{10})(OH)_2$ silicates	dark green to brown to black	3.0*	2.5–3	perfect cleavage in one direction to form flexible sheets
Halite	$NaCl$ halides	colorless, white	2.16	2.5	has a salty taste; dissolves in water; cleaves in three directions
Augite	$(Ca, Na)(Mg, Fe, Al)(Si, Al)_2O_6$ silicates	dark green to black	3.3*	5–6	glassy luster; cleaves in two directions; crystals have 8-sided cross section
Hornblende	$(Ca, Na)_{2-3}(MgFeAl)_5$ $Si_6(SiAl)_2O_{22}(OH)_2$ silicates	dark green to black	3.2*	5–6	glassy luster; cleaves in two directions; crystals have 6-sided cross section
Hematite	Fe_2O_3 oxides	reddish brown to black	5.26	5.5–6.5	metallic luster in crystals; dull luster in earthy variety; dark red streak
Dolomite	$CaMg(CO_3)_2$ carbonates	pink, colorless, white, gray	2.85	3.5–4	does not react to HCl as quickly as calcite; cleaves in three directions
Magnetite	Fe_3O_4 oxides	black	5.18	6	metallic luster; black streak; strongly magnetic
Copper	Cu native elements	copper-red on fresh surface	8.9	2.5–3	metallic luster; fractures; can be easily shaped
Graphite	C native elements	black to gray	2.3	1–2	black to gray streak; marks paper; feels slippery

DataBank

Classification of Major Igneous Rocks

Chemical Composition			Granitic	Andesitic	Basaltic	Ultramafic
Dominant Minerals			Quartz Potassium feldspar Sodium-rich plagioclase feldspar	Amphibole Sodium- and calcium-rich plagioclase feldspar	Pyroxene Calcium-rich plagioclase feldspar	Olivine Pyroxene
T E X T U R E	Coarse-grained		Granite	Diorite	Gabbro	Peridotite
	Fine-grained		Rhyolite	Andesite	Basalt	Komatiite (rare)
	Porphyritic		"Porphyritic" precedes any of the above names whenever there are appreciable phenocrysts.			Uncommon
	Glassy		Obsidian (compact glass) Pumice (frothy glass)			
Rock Color (based on % of dark minerals)			0% to 25%	25% to 45%	45% to 85%	85% to 100%

Classification of Major Metamorphic Rocks

Rock Name	Texture		Grain Size	Comments	Parent Rock
Slate	Increasing Metamorphism	Foliated	Very fine	Smooth dull surfaces	Shale, mudstone, or siltstone
Phyllite			Fine	Breaks along wavey surfaces, glossy sheen	Slate
Schist			Medium to Coarse	Micaceous minerals dominate	Phyllite
Gneiss			Medium to Coarse	Banding of minerals	Schist, granite, or volcanic rocks
Marble		Nonfoliated	Medium to coarse	Interlocking calcite or dolomite grains	Limestone, dolostone
Quartzite			Medium to coarse	Fused quartz grains, massive, very hard	Quartz sandstone
Anthracite			Fine	Shiny black organic rock that fractures	Bituminous coal

Classification of Major Sedimentary Rocks

Clastic Sedimentary Rocks

Texture (grain size)		Sediment Name	Rock Name
Coarse (over 2 mm)		Gravel (rounded fragments)	Conglomerate
		Gravel (angular fragments)	Breccia
Medium (1/16 to 2 mm)		Sand	Sandstone
Fine (1/16 to 1/256 mm)		Mud	Siltstone
Very fine (less than 1/256 mm)		Mud	Shale

Chemical Sedimentary Rocks

Composition	Texture (grain size)	Rock Name	
Calcite, CaCO₃	Fine to coarse crystalline	Crystalline Limestone	
		Travertine	
	Visible shells and shell fragments loosely cemented	Coquina	Biochemical Limestone
	Various size shells and shell fragments cemented with calcite cement	Fossiliferous Limestone	
	Microscopic shells and clay	Chalk	
Quartz, SiO₂	Very fine crystalline	Chert (light colored) Flint (dark colored)	
Gypsum CaSO₄•2H₂O	Fine to coarse crystalline	Rock Gypsum	
Halite, NaCl	Fine to coarse crystalline	Rock Salt	
Altered plant fragments	Fine-grained organic matter	Bituminous Coal	

DataBank

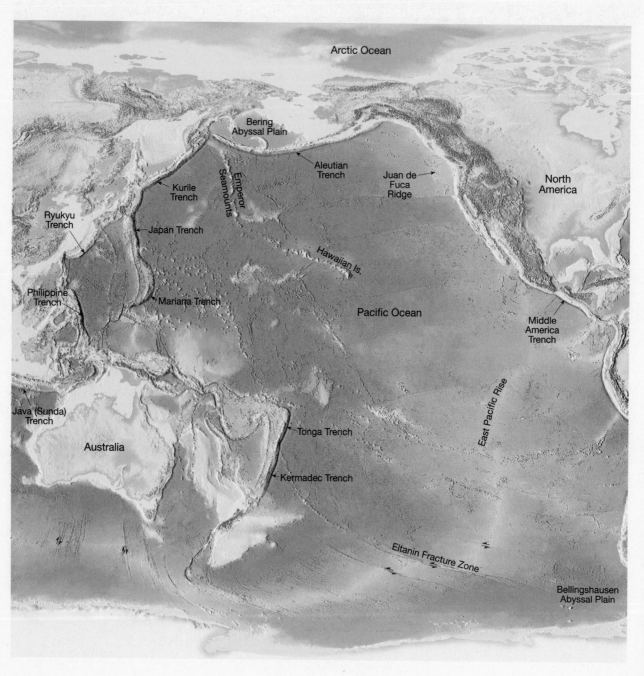

Greenland

Arctic
Mid-Ocean Ridge

Asia

Gibbs
Fracture
Zone

Puerto-Rico
Trench

Atlantic
Ocean

Red Sea
Rift

Demerara
Abyssal Plain

Mid-Atlantic Ridge

Africa

Mid-Indian Ridge

St. Paul
Fracture
Zone

Indian
Ocean

South
America

Peru-Chile
trench

Southwest Indian Ridge

Southeast Indian Ridge

South Sandwich
Trench

Weddell Abyssal Plain

Key: ⇌ transform fault

Spring Sky

To use this chart, hold it up in front of you and turn it so the direction you are facing is at the bottom of the chart. The chart works best at 35° N latitude, but it can be used at other latitudes. It works best at the following dates and times: March 1 at 10 P.M. and April 1 at 8 P.M.

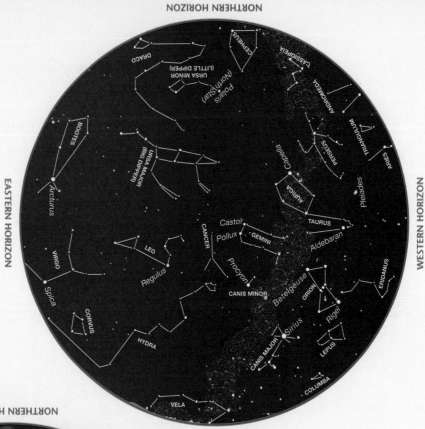

Summer Sky

To use this chart, hold it up in front of you and turn it so the direction you are facing is at the bottom of the chart. The chart works best at 35° N latitude, but it can be used at other latitudes. It works best at the following dates and times: May 15 at 11 P.M. and June 15 at 9 P.M.

Autumn Sky

To use this chart, hold it up in front of you and turn it so the direction you are facing is at the bottom of the chart. The chart works best at 35° N latitude, but it can be used at other latitudes. It works best at the following dates and times: September 1 at 10 P.M., October 1 at 8 P.M., and November 1 at 6 P.M.

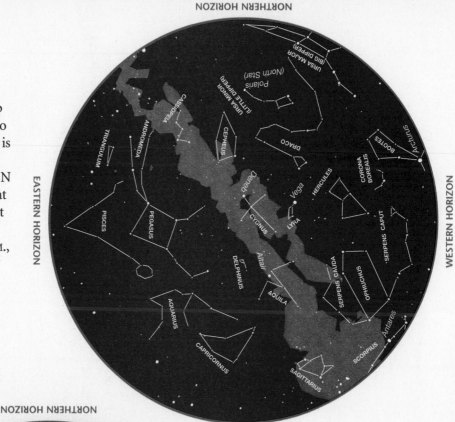

NORTHERN HORIZON

EASTERN HORIZON

WESTERN HORIZON

SOUTHERN HORIZON

URSA MAJOR (BIG DIPPER)
Polaris (North Star)
URSA MINOR (LITTLE DIPPER)
CASSIOPEIA
CEPHEUS
DRACO
BOÖTES
Arcturus
CORONA BOREALIS
HERCULES
Vega
LYRA
CYGNUS
SERPENS CAPUT
Deneb
ANDROMEDA
TRIANGULUM
PISCES
PEGASUS
DELPHINUS
Altair
AQUILA
SERPENS CAUDA
OPHIUCHUS
AQUARIUS
CAPRICORNUS
SAGITTARIUS
SCORPIUS
Antares

Winter Sky

To use this chart, hold it up in front of you and turn it so the direction you are facing is at the bottom of the chart. The chart works best at 35° N latitude, but it can be used at other latitudes. It works best at the following dates and times: December 1 at 10 P.M., January 1 at 8 P.M., and February 1 at 6 P.M.

NORTHERN HORIZON

EASTERN HORIZON

WESTERN HORIZON

SOUTHERN HORIZON

URSA MAJOR (BIG DIPPER)
DRACO
URSA MINOR (LITTLE DIPPER)
Polaris (North Star)
CEPHEUS
CASSIOPEIA
Deneb
CYGNUS
CANCER
Pollux
Castor
GEMINI
Procyon
CANIS MINOR
Capella
AURIGA
PERSEUS
DELPHINUS
Betelgeuse
TAURUS
PLEIADES
ANDROMEDA
TRIANGULUM
PEGASUS
ORION
Aldebaran
CANIS MAJOR
Sirius
Rigel
PISCES
AQUARIUS
CETUS

DataBank

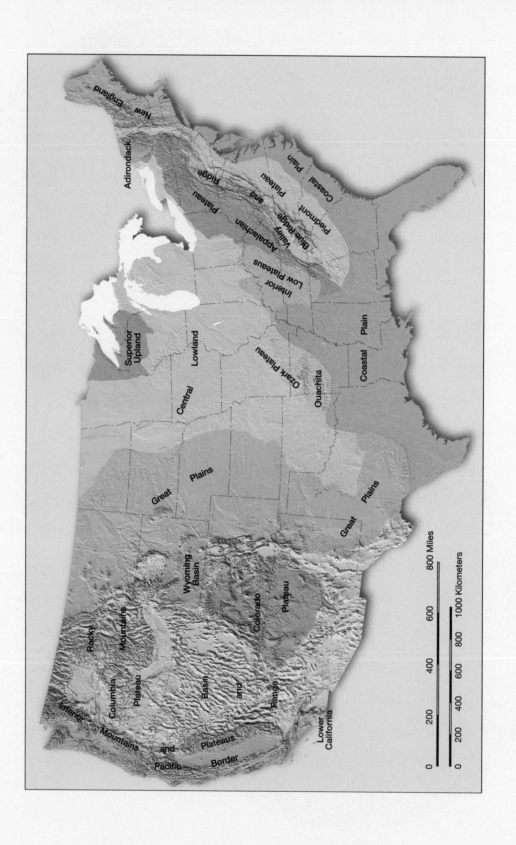

New England

Adirondack

Appalachian Plateau

Valley and Ridge

Blue Ridge

Piedmont

Coastal Plain

Interior Low Plateaus

Superior Upland

Central Lowland

Ozark Plateau

Ouachita

Coastal Plain

Great Plains

Great Plains

Wyoming Basin

Colorado Plateau

Rocky Mountains

Columbia Plateau

Interior Mountains and Plateaus

Basin and Range

Pacific Border

Lower California

800 Miles

1000 Kilometers

0   200   400   600

0   200   400   600   800

Landforms of the Conterminous United States

0	200	400	600	800 Miles

| 0 | 200 | 400 | 600 | 800 | 1000 Kilometers |

Data provided by the U.S. Geological Survey

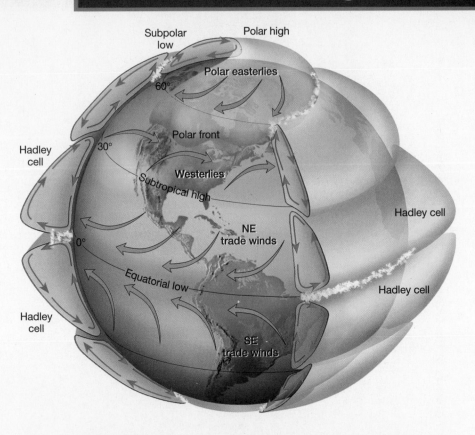

Hertzsprung-Russel Diagram

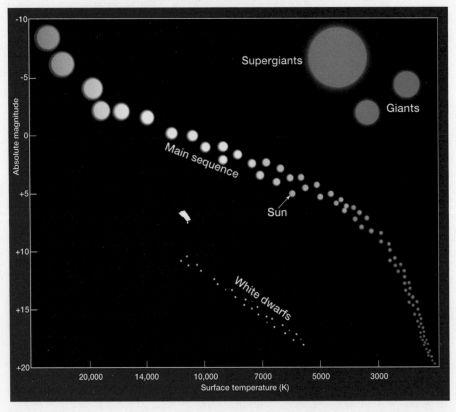

DataBank

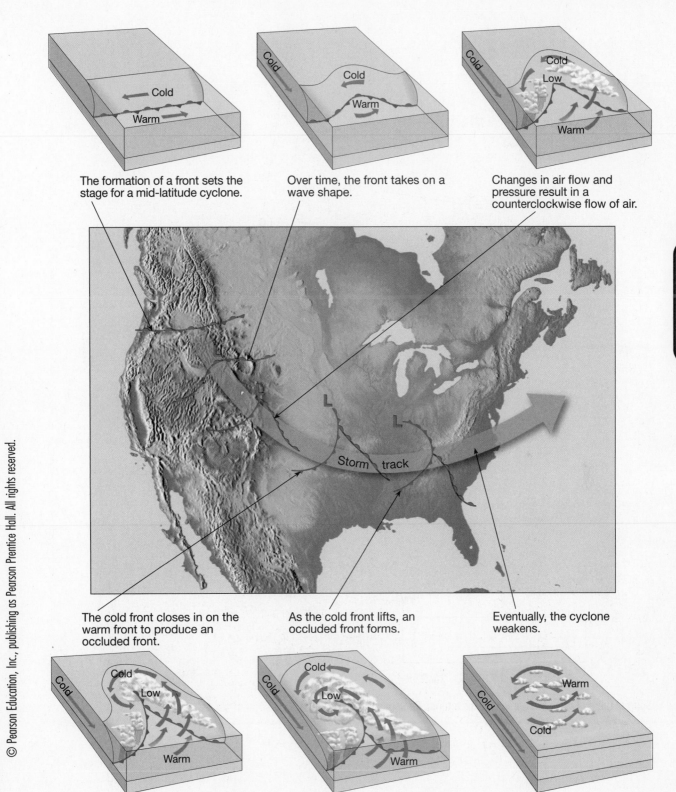

The formation of a front sets the stage for a mid-latitude cyclone.

Over time, the front takes on a wave shape.

Changes in air flow and pressure result in a counterclockwise flow of air.

The cold front closes in on the warm front to produce an occluded front.

As the cold front lifts, an occluded front forms.

Eventually, the cyclone weakens.

DataBank

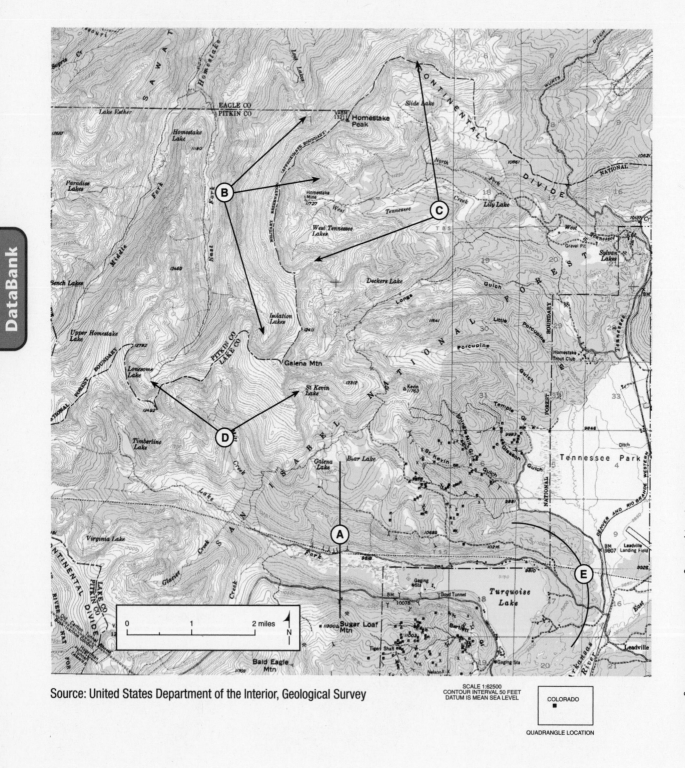

Source: United States Department of the Interior, Geological Survey

SCALE 1:62500
CONTOUR INTERVAL 50 FEET
DATUM IS MEAN SEA LEVEL

COLORADO

QUADRANGLE LOCATION